Young Children's
Mathematics

Cognitively Guided Instruction in Early Childhood Education

Thomas P. Carpenter • Megan L. Franke • Nicholas C. Johnson

Angela Chan Turrou • Anita A. Wager

Includes Online Video

HEINEMANN
Portsmouth, NH

S0-AEB-893

Heinemann
361 Hanover Street
Portsmouth, NH 03801–3912
www.heinemann.com

Offices and agents throughout the world

© 2017 Thomas P. Carpenter, Megan L. Franke, Nicholas C. Johnson, Angela Chan Turrou, and Anita A. Wager

All rights reserved. No part of this book may be reproduced in any form or by any electronic or mechanical means, including information storage and retrieval systems, without permission in writing from the publisher, except by a reviewer, who may quote brief passages in a review.

The authors have dedicated a great deal of time and effort to writing the content of this book, and their written expression is protected by copyright law. We respectfully ask that you do not adapt, reuse, or copy anything on third-party (whether for-profit or not-for-profit) lesson-sharing websites. As always, we're happy to answer any questions you may have.

—Heinemann Publishers

"Dedicated to Teachers" is a trademark of Greenwood Publishing Group, Inc.

The preparation of this book was supported in part by grants from the National Science Foundation (Grant # 144-PRJ38LG) and the Heising-Simons Foundation. The opinions expressed in this book do not necessarily reflect the position, policy, or endorsement of the National Science Foundation or the Heising-Simons Foundation.

Library of Congress Cataloging-in-Publication Data
Names: Carpenter, Thomas P.
Title: Young children's mathematics : cognitively guided instruction in early
    childhood education / Thomas P. Carpenter [and four others].
Description: Portsmouth, NH : Heinemann, 2016 | Includes bibliographical
    references.
Identifiers: LCCN 2016030216 | ISBN 9780325078120
Subjects: LCSH: Mathematics—Study and teaching (Early childhood) | Counting.
    | Early childhood education.
Classification: LCC QA135.6 .Y68 2016 | DDC 372.7/049—dc23

LC record available at https://lccn.loc.gov/2016030216

Editor: Katherine Bryant
Production Editor: Sonja S. Chapman
Cover and interior designs: Suzanne Heiser
Typesetter: Kim Arney
Manufacturing: Steve Bernier

Printed in the United States of America on acid-free paper

21   20   19   RWP   4   5

CONTENTS

ACKNOWLEDGMENTS

We are enormously grateful to the teachers and children whose ideas made this book possible. We wish to thank the teachers who helped us to understand what early childhood experiences can be when we listen carefully to young children as they express their mathematical thinking, and the many children who allowed us to participate as they shared their thinking with their teachers and with one another. We are also grateful to our colleagues Joan Case, Victoria Jacobs, Anne Karabon, Courtney Koestler, and Amy Noelle Parks for their thoughtful feedback on earlier drafts of the manuscript. Finally, we wish to thank Katherine Bryant, Sonja Chapman, and their team at Heinemann for their insight, patience, and guidance throughout the writing and production process.

1

Introduction

Young children are naturally curious and observant, and they enter school ready to connect their rich informal understandings about the world around them to their experiences in classrooms. We notice this as they explore the materials in the classroom, as they play together on the playground, and as they interact with each other on a day-to-day basis. Children may not know they are doing mathematics or engaging in mathematically related conversation and play, but mathematics is an integral part of their daily lives from a young age.

In the block area:

"I'm going to build a tower!"

"Me too!"

"I'm going to put 10 blocks in my tower!"

"I'm going to put 20 blocks in mine! Mine is going to be bigger!"

"Then I'm going to put more!"

In the art center two children are divvying up crayons:

"We have to share them!"
"Okay. You get one, I get one, you get one, I get one, you get one, I get one."
"Let's keep going until they are all gone."
"And you and me have the same number."

On the playground a group of children are counting as they scoop sand into the bucket:

"94, 95, 96, 97, 98, 99 . . . 100!"

We are particularly impressed by the ways children spontaneously demonstrate their excitement for numbers and their understanding of relationships involving quantities from an early age, and how teachers leverage these opportunities to engage children in doing mathematics. Studies have shown that during informal interactions with other children (e.g., on the playground, in centers, during play), children's play involves a wide range of mathematics.

A primary goal of preschool and kindergarten mathematics instruction is for students to develop basic number concepts. Learning to count is one of the earliest formal mathematical activities that young children engage in, and counting has a central role in young children's mathematical thinking throughout preschool and the primary grades. Children enter school with at least some understanding of how to count and with an emerging awareness of how to use their understanding of counting and number to begin to solve problems.

Our research has shown how productive it can be for teachers to attend to and build from children's already existing rich understanding about mathematics. As we spend time in preschool and kindergarten classrooms, we see this happening in myriad ways, including during the daily routines that teachers set up in their classrooms. For instance, children may count from 1 to 20 as they wash their hands, count the number of paper plates they will need so each child gets one, and count each student as they are lining up to go outside and to return back in. They may use several different strategies to compare how many more children are wearing long sleeves than short sleeves or how many children are absent that day.

As we spend time in classrooms with young children, we notice the remarkable ways teachers already engage students to build their mathematical understanding. Ms. Quezada counts library books with her preschoolers each time they return their backpacks to the classroom, varying the kinds of counting support she provides to each child. Ms. Torres circulates the room as children play and responds to Carlos' request for more food coloring at the water table with a simple question of "How many drops do you want today?" Ms. Vergara notices two of her students looking at each other's collection of bottle caps and asks them how many bottle caps they would have if they put them all together.

Teachers of young children have already found productive ways to leverage the mathematics within daily routines, informal play, and structured activities. Capitalizing on these opportunities allows children to connect their knowledge about the world to the learning of mathematics in school, to see school as connected to what they know about the world rather than as separate from it. These teachers' interactions with their students and our experiences in their classrooms have demonstrated time and again that the details of children's mathematical ideas matter, and that noticing and building from children's thinking creates powerful learning opportunities.

Teacher Reflection

I used to be someone who was intimidated by math. I thought of math as a sitting activity. Learning about children's thinking has helped me to see that throughout the day there are opportunities for teachable moments for math. Now when we read we do a lot of body movement and counting. I find that there can be so much math language that I can add using any children's book. I realize I'm using math during circle time, free choice time, transition. Math is everywhere!

—**Patty Romo,** *preschool teacher*

Focusing on Children's Mathematical Thinking

This book is a companion to *Children's Mathematics: Cognitively Guided Instruction*[1] and is driven by the same guiding principles of teaching and learning mathematics. Learning about the development of children's mathematical thinking and attending

---

1. See reference at end of chapter.

to the details of children's counting and problem-solving strategies can support you to recognize and build from children's intuitive understandings of mathematics. Focusing on what children already know and can do mathematically allows you to position them as competent and to support them to communicate their understandings. Centering children's thinking in your decision making as a teacher allows you to purposefully design or adapt instructional tasks and to intervene in the moment in ways that are responsive to the needs and understandings of each child.

This book will support you to notice and make sense of young children's mathematical thinking, and provide you with examples of how teachers have created opportunities to build from children's mathematical ideas in their instruction. Throughout this book we focus on the ways that children count collections of objects and use counting to solve problems. The development of understanding that we illustrate across chapters and examples is not particular to certain ages, but spans the entirety of early childhood. In Chapter 2, we detail the most critical principles that support the development of counting. In Chapter 3, we discuss cases of children acquiring and applying counting principles, focusing on what children *do* know about counting as they demonstrate emerging understanding of the principles.

In the following chapters, we discuss how children apply their emerging counting skills to solve problems. It turns out that young children are remarkably successful in intuitively applying their counting skills to solve a variety of problems in a number of different contexts. In Chapter 4, we look specifically at how counting can be extended into problem solving, the types of problems children can solve, and the strategies they use to solve them. In Chapter 5, we highlight the spaces in which counting and problem solving emerge in classrooms. In Chapter 6 we discuss how the strategies described in Chapter 4 are extended to solve arithmetic story problems. Chapter 7 examines how teachers engage with children and support them to develop their counting and problem-solving strategies. Chapter 8 draws on what we know about children's mathematical thinking inside and outside of school and looks at how ideas of children's thinking and informal practices can be used to bridge children's worlds of home and school. Chapter 9 returns us to an examination of children's thinking and looks forward to place value and how the ideas of grouping naturally arise as children extend counting to base-ten number concepts. Chapter 10 draws together some of the major themes developed throughout the book.

We are excited to share what we have been learning from teachers in early childhood settings in a way that helps you navigate the details of children's mathematical thinking and consider how you might respond as a teacher. As we share examples, we do not prescribe particular ways of teaching, using curricula, or interacting with children. We believe, however, that teachers' decision-making can be informed by a perspective that focuses on how children's learning develops, and how the experiences that produce learning shape the nature of what is learned. We think it is productive to consider, for example, the understandings we can expect children to construct by drawing from their intuitive understandings of mathematics and the world, versus those that involve simply adopting formal mathematical conventions. This goes beyond debates about telling versus not telling, discovery versus direct instruction, play-based versus structured. Teachers may be intentional in their decision-making and draw from many different approaches in supporting students to learn. What we advocate in this book is not a particular way of teaching, but a stance that looks for what children know, and centers children's ideas and sense making in the teaching and learning of mathematics. A focus on children's thinking can provide a starting point for creating classroom spaces where varied ways of knowing and participating can emerge.

Getting Started

As you make your way through this book, we hope that you carve out opportunities to connect the reading to your day-to-day work with children. Although we attempt to provide examples of children engaging in mathematics in this book, we find in our work with teachers that the most powerful learning occurs when interacting directly with children—providing a variety of mathematical opportunities, noticing what they are doing, asking questions, and so on. We invite you to regularly try out ideas with children as you read the book and to reflect (especially with colleagues!) upon what you are experiencing.

(continues)

Some suggestions for getting started on diving into young children's mathematical thinking:

- Give a child a collection of objects and observe how the child counts. Ask them to count for you more than once. Try again with a different collection of objects.
- Pose a story problem to a child and ask them to solve it without telling them how to do so. Encourage them to use fingers or counters to help them think through the story. Ask, "How did you figure that out?"
- Observe children playing together both indoors and outdoors. See if you notice any mathematical ideas arising in their play.

Reference

Carpenter, T. P., E. Fennema, M. L. Franke, S. B. Empson, and L. W. Levi. 2015. *Children's Mathematics: Cognitively Guided Instruction*. 2nd ed. Portsmouth, NH: Heinemann.

2

Foundational Concepts of Counting and Number

Mohammad is asked to count a collection of 8 plastic bears. He counts out loud, "1, 2, 3, 4, 5, 6, 7, 8." As he counts he touches each bear exactly once, and coordinates his saying of number words with his touching of the bears. After he finishes counting, Mohammad is asked how many bears he has, and he responds, "8."

CLIP 2.1 Mohammad counts 8 bears
http://hein.pub/YCM2.1

When accomplished easily, as Mohammad does in the example above, counting can appear to be quite simple. However, unpacking the details of what children do as they count reveals their understanding of a complex, interconnected process—a process that is anything but simple. While young children's ability to count accurately is often still emerging, the details of their actions demonstrate an intuitive sense of the intricacies of counting. Even when their thinking may seem wrong or incomplete, there is often an underlying understanding of the core mathematical ideas of counting that can be productively built upon.

The importance of learning to count cannot be overstated. Counting is the foundation upon which number concepts and skills are built. The ability to count accurately, flexibly, and with understanding supports children's future success in mathematics. Opportunities to count abound in children's daily lives, and counting can provide an ideal activity for connecting home and school learning experiences. Recognizing what children know about counting can help you build on the knowledge that they have acquired outside of school and help them connect their in-school and out-of-school learning.

In this chapter, we discuss the basic principles of counting and the related process of subitizing. Our aim is to first offer a clear articulation of the counting principles to provide a framework to support you in noticing and interpreting the details of what children do as they learn to count. Chapter 3 provides a variety of examples that illustrate a range of ways that these principles develop. We encourage you to read these two chapters together, moving back and forth between them. Understanding the counting principles will support you to see how they emerge as children count, and examining what children do will provide deeper understanding of the mathematical ideas embedded within the counting principles.

Fundamental Counting Principles

Learning to count involves more than learning to recite a sequence of number names; it also involves being able to use the sequence of number names to count collections of objects. For counting a collection of objects to make any sense, two people counting the same collection need to arrive at the same result. (We refer to counting *objects* for simplicity, though we can also count sounds, movements, sequenced events, and measures for which distinct parts cannot be isolated such as weight, length, or area.) This depends on a number of principles that govern the use of counting. These principles are summarized in the following list.

Counting Principles

- There is an **ordered sequence of counting numbers**, and numbers are always assigned to items in a collection in the same order starting with one.
- **The one-to-one principle**. Exactly one number from the counting sequence is assigned to each item in the collection.
- **The cardinal principle.** The last number in the counting sequence assigned to the collection represents the number of objects in the collection.

Any finite collection of objects can be counted. As long as these principles are followed, counting will assign a unique number to a collection that will be the same no matter what order the items are counted in.

Learning the Sequence of Number Names

Learning to recite the standard sequence of number names is somewhat different from children's other language learning experiences. Most words are used in various combinations. One of the fundamental principles of counting is that the sequence of number names is invariant. Counting must be done by saying the number names in a fixed order. Thus, children not only need to learn the number names, they also need to understand the principle that counting numbers appear in a fixed sequence. They also need to understand that numbers are not repeated in the counting sequence, and they have to learn the specific order of number names in that sequence. Young children may learn some of these features of counting before others. For example, some children may learn some number names, but not understand that the numbers follow a sequence. Other children may understand that numbers should follow a fixed sequence but not know what the correct sequence is.

The Base-Ten Number System

Fortunately, learning to count does not require learning an entirely new name for each number. Rather, learning to count involves memorizing a relatively small sequence of number names and learning a few rules for generating larger number names. We have a base-ten number system, which essentially means that once we have more than 10 objects to count, we group by tens and count the tens and the leftover ones. When we get 10 tens, we group into hundreds and count the hundreds. The process continues with thousands, ten thousands, hundred thousands, millions, and so on. Children's understanding of the base-ten number system is discussed in Chapter 9.

Spoken Numbers Versus Written Numerals

There is a major difference between the way we speak number names and the way we write numerals. With spoken number words, we specifically name the groupings. For 342, we say "three hundred forty-two," designating each of the groups of hundred, ten, one, and so forth. In English and other European languages, the words used to designate the groups become explicit after we get to 100. We specifically say "three hundred," "five thousand," "forty thousand," and the like. The names for the groups of ten are not quite so obvious. We say "twenty" and "fifty" instead of "two tens" and " five tens." The teens are even less principled. With numbers beyond 20, at least the tens come before the ones. With teens that is not true. We say "thirteen," "fourteen," "fifteen," which, by the way, sound a lot like "thirty," "forty," "fifty." Furthermore, *eleven* and *twelve* are entirely new words with little relation to *one* and *two*.

In most Asian languages, on the other hand, the number of tens, hundreds, and so forth are explicitly designated using the number words for the numbers 1 to 9 (see Figure 2.1). For example, the English equivalent of 27 is spoken as "two-ten-seven," meaning 2 tens and 7 ones. This makes learning Chinese number names a great deal easier than learning English number names.

With written numerals, we use a place value system to designate the groups of ten, hundred, and so forth. Thus, 342 means 3 hundreds, 4 tens, and 2 ones. The numerals 342 and 234 represent different numbers, because the 2, 3, and 4 are in different places. We use zeros to maintain the place value when there are no tens, hundreds, and the like. Thus, 302 represents 3 hundreds and 2 ones, and 302 represents a different number than 32. With spoken number words, we do not have to say "zero tens" to maintain the place as we do with written numerals. Because we name the groups, we can just say "three hundred two."

Essentially, English-speaking children have to memorize the number names for numbers from 1 to 12. The teen numbers (13–19) have roots in the numbers from 3 to 9, which can provide some support for learning them, but there are quirks in the language. *Fourteen*, *sixteen*, *seventeen*, *eighteen*, and *nineteen* essentially add *teen* (standing for *ten*) onto *four*, *six*, *seven*, *eight*, and *nine*. But *thirteen* and *fifteen*

Numeral	Chinese	English	Spanish*	Hmong
1	Yi	One	Uno	Ib
2	Er	Two	Dos	Ob
3	San	Three	Tres	Peb
4	Si	Four	Cuatro	Nplaub
5	Wu	Five	Cinco	Ntsib
6	Liu	Six	Seis	Rau
7	Qi	Seven	Siete	Xya
8	Ba	Eight	Ocho	Yim
9	Jiu	Nine	Nueve	Cuaj
10	Shi	Ten	Diez	Kaum
11	Shi-yi	Eleven	Once	Kaum-ib
12	Shi-er	Twelve	Doce	Kaum-ob
13	Shi-san	Thirteen	Trece	Kaum-peb
14	Shi-si	Fourteen	Catorce	Kaum-plaub
15	Shi-wu	Fifteen	Quince	Kaum-tsib
16	Shi-liu	Sixteen	Dieciséis	Kaum-rau
17	Shi-qi	Seventeen	Diecisiete	Kaum-xya
18	Shi-ba	Eighteen	Dieciocho	Kaum-yim
19	Shi-ju	Nineteen	Diecinueve	Kaum-cuaj
20	Er-shi	Twenty	Veinte	Neesnkaum
21	Er-shi-yi	Twenty-one	Veintiuno	Neesnkaum-ib
22	Er-shi-er	Twenty-two	Veintidós	Neesnkaum-ob
23	Er-shi-san	Twenty-three	Veintitrés	Neesnkaum-peb
30	San-shi	Thirty	Treinta	Peb caug
40	Si-shi	Forty	Cuarenta	Plaub caug
50	Wu-shi	Fifty	Cincuenta	Tsib caug
60	Liu-shi	Sixty	Sesenta	Rau caum
70	Qi-shi	Seventy	Setenta	Xya caum
80	Ba-shi	Eighty	Ochenta	Yim caum
90	Ju-shi	Ninety	Noventa	Cuaj caum
100	Bai	One hundred	Cien	Pau

*Alternative spellings and pronunciations for some Spanish number names are used in different countries.

Figure 2.1 Counting words in different languages

are a little different. As a consequence, some children may say "fiveteen" instead of "fifteen." Interestingly, this seems to represent an attempt to make some sense of the counting sequence and may be made by children who have some insight at least into the patterns represented by the counting sequence and are trying to make sense of counting rather than just memorize a rote sequence of meaningless words.

Thus, for many children, learning to count from 1 to 20 involves learning a sequence of number names for which they may or may not see a recurring pattern in the teens. After 20, things start to make more sense and generative rules can be applied. To count beyond 20, children need only to apply their knowledge of counting from 1 to 9 for the numbers between decade numbers (20, 30, 40, and so on). The most likely place for errors to occur is when the count gets to a new decade (*thirty-ten* rather than *forty*). Furthermore, the English decade number names are not transparent, which presents an additional challenge for children learning to count in English (particularly for young children who have not mastered phonics or spelling). As with the teens, twenty has only a slight resemblance to two, and thirty and fifty are marginally related to three and five. The other decade numbers incorporate the corresponding number names of numbers less than 10, but *-ty* (as in *sixty*) is used in place of *ten*. There is a pattern, but the language does not clearly support the conceptual notion of groups of ten.

Counting Collections of Objects: The One-to-One and Cardinal Principles

If counting only entailed learning a sequence of number names, it would have little relevance beyond its use in activities like hide-and-seek. One of the reasons counting is so important is that it allows us to determine the number of objects in any given collection and to use this knowledge to solve a variety of problems. The one-to-one and cardinal principles are critical to this process.

One-to-One Principle

The one-to-one principle says that there must be a one-to-one correspondence between numbers in the counting sequence and the objects in the collection that is counted so that each object is counted exactly once. In other words, the numbers in the counting sequence are assigned to each object in the collection until all the objects in the collection have been assigned a number and no two objects have been assigned the same number. The assignment of numbers starts with 1, and subsequent numbers in the sequence are assigned to objects in the order in which the numbers appear in the counting sequence.

In counting any collection of objects, children need to keep track of which objects have been counted and which remain to be counted to be able to make a one-to-one match between the number names in the counting sequence and the objects in the collection. One possibility is to keep track of which objects have been counted and which still need to be counted by moving the objects that have been counted so that they are separate from the objects to be counted. Counting can also be facilitated by arranging objects in a straight line or some other organized configuration. If the objects are in a straight line, it is possible to start at the left (or the right) and count the objects in order. The objects to the left of the last counted object have been counted, and the objects to the right are yet to be counted.

In either case, it is important that children understand why they are lining up or grouping objects. Children may line up or group objects to count because they have observed adults or other children doing it without really understanding why. Even when objects are grouped or lined up, some young children violate the one-to-one principle. They may double count an object, they may skip objects, or they may simply recite the counting words as they move their finger along the row of objects without attempting to match counting words with objects.

For example, two children are each counting a collection of 8 buttons. Elise systematically touches each button as she counts it and moves the button she has counted to a pile that is separate from the uncounted buttons. This allows her to keep track of the buttons she has counted and those yet to be counted, so she counts each button exactly once. Jesse, on the other hand, lines the buttons up in a row, but as he counts, he simply runs his finger along the row, not matching a counting word with a button. He winds up with a count of 6.

Cardinal Principle

The goal of counting a group of objects is to find the number of objects in the collection. The cardinal principle says that the last number name recited in counting a collection of objects represents the number of objects counted.

Some young children who can accurately apply the one-to-one principle in counting a collection of objects do not understand the cardinal principle. They essentially equate the act of counting with the question "how many?" The process of counting is the response to the question. If they have counted a collection and are asked how many objects are in the collection, they may recount the collection, or say a single random number word. Other children may not recognize that the last number in the counting sequence represents the number of objects in the entire collection. They may think that the last number counted refers only to the last object. For example, if they have counted a collection of 5 markers and are asked to show what the five refers to, they may point to the last object counted. Thus, when assessing a child's counting skills, it is important to ask further questions such as, "How many objects are there?" and not assume that because a child has counted correctly that they understand what the count tells them. On the other hand, some children may demonstrate that they know the last number in a count represents the number of objects in a collection before they have learned the standard counting sequence or before they consistently apply the one-to-one principle.

Other Important Counting Ideas

What Gets Counted

Although it is relatively straightforward to figure out what to count when a collection consists of similar objects, in some instances decisions have to be made about what the units are that get counted. For example, children can have difficulty when some of the things to be counted are broken apart, but the goal is to count the number of whole items. For example, consider counting the number of cakes for a school party where several of the cakes have been cut into pieces. A distinction needs to be made between the pieces and the whole cakes, and each piece and each whole cake are not counted as the same. But young children may not make this distinction. If there are 4 whole cakes and a fifth cake that has been cut into 6 pieces, some children may count each individual cake and piece the same to get a total of 10 cakes.

Counting Collections and Making Collections

Up to this point, we have talked about counting collections of objects, but actually there are two quite different counting activities involving counting collections of objects, and it is important that children have ample opportunity to engage in both types of counting activity. The same basic counting principles apply in both cases, but children may be competent at one and have difficulty with the other. In one case, the goal is to find the number of objects in a given collection. In the second, the goal is to generate a collection of a given size. For example, a child might be asked to put 5 blocks in a pile. Note that constructing a set of a given size explicitly depends on an understanding of the cardinal principle.

Comparing Collections

Counting not only tells you how many objects are in a given collection, it can also be used to compare two collections. An important application of counting entails recognizing that a collection with a higher count has more things in it than a collection with a lower count.

Counting Collections and Ordering the Objects in a Collection

Up to this point we have focused on using counting to determine the number of objects in a collection, but counting can also be used to order a collection of objects (first, second, third, . . .). We use the terms *cardinal number* and *ordinal number* to distinguish between these two uses of number. The distinction is important. In one case, counting assigns a number to the entire collection (there are 12 children in the class); in the other, a number is assigned to each object in the collection (Jan is first in line, Ramona is second, and so on). In the case of cardinal numbers, it does not matter in what order the objects are counted. The result of the count should be the same. On the other hand, with ordinal numbers, establishing an ordered sequence is the whole point of the exercise, and many different ordered sequences are possible for a given collection. We are not suggesting you use the terms *cardinal number* or *ordinal number* with your students, but the distinction between them is important.

Number and Numeral

Another important distinction is between the actual number of objects in a collection and the symbol used to represent that number. Technically the name for the written symbol is *numeral*, and at one time even primary grade mathematics books made a point of emphasizing the use of the "appropriate" term. It was not proper to say, "Write the number 5 on your paper." Instead, you were to say, "Write the numeral 5 on your paper." But most adults use the word *number* when actually referring to numerals. We are less pedantic today about the use of the word *numeral*, but the distinction between *numeral* and *number* is important for teachers to keep in mind. Once again we are not suggesting that you use the term *numeral* with your class. We introduce the term here to clarify the distinction between numbers and the symbols used to represent them.

Subitizing

For small collections of objects, children can directly perceive the number of objects in the collection without having to count. This process, called *subitizing*, is thought to play a fundamental role in the development of children's basic concept of number, and even infants are capable of distinguishing between small collections containing 3 or fewer objects.

The ability to immediately visualize the number of objects in a collection is usually limited to collections containing 4 or fewer objects. Douglas Clements (1999) calls this ability *perceptual subitizing*—the number of objects is directly perceived as a single unit. However, children often can identify the number of objects in larger collections by building from this ability. They may identify the number of objects by partitioning the collection into smaller groups that are within their subitizing range. For example, children may recognize that there are 5 objects in a collection by mentally partitioning the collection into a group of 3 and a group of 2. It is important to recognize that for a child to then arrive at a total of 5, the child must not only subitize the 3 and the 2, but must also have a way of combining the two quantities to find a total. Clements calls this process *conceptual subitizing* to distinguish it from *perceptual subitizing*. Conceptual subitizing can be facilitated if the configuration of objects supports such a grouping, as illustrated in Figure 2.2.

Children also may immediately recognize common configurations such as those that appear on dice, dominos, or playing cards. Some common configurations are illustrated in Figure 2.3. Notice that in these patterns the marks are generally organized in groups of 4 or fewer so children can perceptually subitize the number of items in the subgroups.

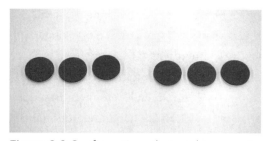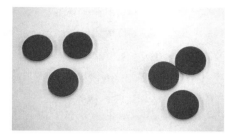

Figure 2.2 Configurations that might support conceptual subitizing

There appears to be relatively little change in children's ability to perceptually subitize, and most adults cannot perceptually subitize collections of much more than 4 objects. Some children and adults may appear to perceptually subitize larger collections, but they generally do so by rapidly recognizing subgroups even though they may not be aware that they are doing so. As a consequence, little is to be gained by attempting to help children to perceptually subitize larger collections. On the other hand, breaking numbers apart is a critical feature of developing number sense at all levels, and partitioning collections to conceptually subitize may represent an early manifestation of this ability.

Children also learn to recognize finger patterns so that they do not have to actually count the fingers that they may have raised on one or both hands (see Figure 2.4). Initially, they may recognize the number of fingers raised on one hand, but with time and experience they learn to recognize

Figure 2.3 Common patterns that children may immediately recognize without counting

Figure 2.4 A child's finger pattern for 7

finger patterns involving both hands. When children count on their fingers, they generally raise all the fingers on one hand before using fingers on the other hand. As a consequence, children are generally more familiar with a finger pattern that is represented by 5 fingers on one hand and additional fingers on the other hand than a related pattern in some other configuration. For example, children might have an easier time recognizing a pattern of 5 fingers on one hand and 2 on the other hand than a pattern of 4 fingers on one hand and 3 on the other. Finger patterns can play an important role in children's use of counting strategies to solve problems, so supporting children's ability to immediately recognize finger patterns can pay dividends as children begin to apply their counting ability.

Not all children are familiar with the same finger patterns. Different people use different finger patterns to represent small numbers. For example, in some countries people consistently use the thumb and index finger to represent the number 2 and are confused if someone holds up the index finger and middle finger for 2, even though just 2 fingers are extended.

Conclusion

A broad general goal of mathematics instruction at all levels is to encourage students to learn to mathematize their everyday experiences. Counting provides a means for young children to mathematize their experiences. Learning to count is the foundation on which number ideas develop. In this chapter we have identified fundamental principles that children must know to count accurately. To develop understanding of these principles, it is important that children be given ample opportunity to count collections of objects and to construct collections containing a given number of objects. In the next chapter we look at some ways in which these counting principles develop in young children.

Questions for Further Reflection

1. Can you think of ways in which the difference between how we say and write numbers may confuse children? What errors might they make in writing the numeral for a spoken number word?

2. How would you say 2,046 in English using the same principle that is used with Chinese number names?

3. How are Spanish number words alike and different from English number words?

4. How many tens are in 426?

5. What might you look for to decide whether a child is using the one-to-one principle? What tasks might you give, and what questions might you ask?

6. What might you look for to decide whether a child understands the cardinal principle? What tasks might you give, and what questions might you ask?

7. What tasks might you give and what questions might you ask to find out whether a child understands that the order in which items are counted does not matter as long as the child uses the one-to-one principle?

8. Consider what it would look like if a child counting 12 objects knew or did not know each of the counting principles. Can you show what that would look like?

References and Further Reading

The principles discussed in this chapter appear throughout the literature on children's learning basic number concepts. This chapter drew heavily on the work of Doug Clements, Karen Fuson, Rochelle Gellman, and Herb Ginsburg. Specific references for their work follow.

Clements, D. H. 1999. "Subitizing: What Is It? Why Teach It?" *Teaching Children Mathematics* (March): 400–405.

Clements, D. H., and J. Sarama. 2007. "Early Childhood Mathematics Learning." In *Second Handbook of Research on Mathematics Teaching and Learning*, edited by F. K. Lester, 461–555. Reston, VA: National Council of Teachers of Mathematics.

Fuson, K. C. 1988. *Children's Counting and Concepts of Number.* New York: Springer-Verlag.

Fuson, K. C., and Y. Kwon. 1991. "Chinese Based Regular and European Irregular Systems of Number Words: The Disadvantages for English Speaking Children." In *Language and Mathematical Education*, edited by K. Derkin and B. Shire, 211–26. Milton Keynes, England: Open University Press.

Gellman, R., and C. R. Galistell. 1978. *The Child's Understanding of Number.* Cambridge, MA: Harvard University Press.

Ginsburg, H. P. 1977. *Children's Arithmetic.* Austin, TX: Pro-ed.

3

The Development of Children's Counting

At this age level if you give anything to count, count, count, they are building up a lot of different math components that I didn't realize were available for that activity.

—Monica Quezada, preschool teacher

For me it's just learning math with them as well. They are showing me what they know, what they can do, and I'm just taking that information and applying it to help them be successful and want to learn more about math.

—Johanna Sanchez-Aviles, preschool teacher

Children like to count collections. We saw in Chapter 2 that as children count collections of objects, they are provided with opportunities to engage with and learn fundamental counting principles. Chapter 3 provides a series of scenarios that illustrate how counting skills and understanding develop. The examples describe a variety of situations that are likely to occur in early childhood classrooms: young children, invited to count collections of objects, often demonstrate emerging understanding of the counting principles. We discuss the ways teachers support the development of counting skills and understanding in more detail in Chapter 7.

When thinking about how children's counting develops, there are four big ideas to keep in mind:

- Details matter when we look for what students know about counting.
- Students can have more counting understanding than we see in a given moment.
- Counting principles do not emerge in a set sequence.
- Counting principles emerge concurrently.

No matter where children are in their understanding of the number sequence, one-to-one correspondence, or the cardinal principle, they can extend their emerging understandings by counting collections of objects. When engaging in counting, a child may not yet draw on all of the principles and may not arrive at a correct total, but the details of what they do will show you that they have some knowledge of how to count. Watching and listening to children's counting will help you see what a child knows and what they still need to learn. Watching and listening over many interactions will provide a more complete picture of what a child understands. The details of what children do and say will help you to make instructional decisions that build on children's emerging understandings and support them to learn more. You will see in this chapter what details to watch and listen for and how those details can help you.

The chapter examines the development of children's understanding of counting: learning the sequence of number names, applying the one-to-one and cardinal principles, counting the entire collection, and organizing the collection. Use of the counting principles will emerge in different ways for different children. Some will learn the counting sequence well before developing one-to-one correspondence, and others will develop one-to-one correspondence before knowing the counting sequence well. Partial understandings of one principle can support a child's learning of the other principles. For example, working on one-to-one correspondence while counting a collection will support children to use what they know about the counting sequence.

The sections of this chapter detail both how children think and how to support their understanding of the counting principles. The final section brings these ideas together to show how the counting principles develop concurrently and how you as a teacher, in attending to the details of children's counting with different objects at different times, can capture what the child knows about the counting principles and use counting collections to support their ongoing learning.

Learning the Counting Sequence

In Chapter 2, we laid out what is entailed in learning the counting sequence. We highlighted that memorizing a set of number words is only a small part of learning to count. Children not only need to learn the number names; they also need to (a) understand that counting numbers appear in a fixed sequence, (b) recognize that numbers are not repeated in the counting sequence, (c) learn the specific order of number names in the counting sequence, and (d) develop an understanding of the structure of the counting sequence (e.g., the repetition of 0–9 with each shift in decade number). Young children may learn some of these features of counting before others; *attending to the details* of how the child currently counts can provide information about what the child understands about the counting sequence.

It can seem that one minute a child has the sequence all figured out, and the next they are repeating number words when they count. Another child may first count in what sounds like a jumbled sequence and then count the same collection again with a correct sequence. This is all part of learning. These miscounts do not mean the child does not know anything about the counting sequence; they just may not yet be able to use what they know consistently. Where, what, and who children are counting with as well as how they are feeling that day will shape how they count. As children become more comfortable with themselves as counters and gain more knowledge and confidence in their counting, they will more consistently show their understanding of the counting sequence.

CLIP 3.1 Miley's counting sequence
http://hein.pub/YCM3.1

CLIP 3.2 Miley counts pennies
http://hein.pub/YCM3.2

Some Common Situations

When children begin to count, often they *know few counting words* and *don't know that the numbers follow a sequence*. For example, in counting toy cars during play, Devon counts "1, 3, 6, 3" and then counts them again saying "1, 6, 3, 2." Devon shows he knows some number words (*one*, *two*, *three*, and *six*) but in this instance does not show that the number words occur in a sequence.

Some children will count *using the correct number words in the correct order, but may skip a number or two*. When asked to count a set of pencils, Cam counts "1, 2, 3, 4, 5, 6, 7, 10." Although Cam skips the numbers 8 and 9, his count reveals that he is developing some understanding of the counting sequence. Cam knows there is a sequence and knows the correct sequence to 7.

Sometimes when children do not know the correct sequence or all of the number names, they count the correct order to a point and then continue by *reusing some piece of the counting sequence*. For example, when asked to count a set of 14 crayons, Lydia counts "1, 2, 3, 4, 5, 6, 7, 8, 9, 10, 8, 9, 10, 8." Lydia has the correct counting sequence to 10, then continues by reusing 8, 9, 10 repeatedly until she completes counting the entire collection of crayons. Lydia shows a great deal of understanding in her counting. She shows that she knows ten number words, knows that counting involves using the number words in a specific sequence, and that she must continue counting until she has counted the entire set of objects. Furthermore, Lydia's reuse of part of the number sequence shows an emerging understanding of the idea that there is a structure of the number sequence that governs how aspects of the sequence repeat. Even if children cannot correctly use the counting sequence past 10, they may have heard counting and participated in counting in ways that help them start to make sense of the principle that there is repetition in the counting sequence. Lydia does not display a complete understanding of the counting structure, but the details of her counting reveals that she uses the idea that a structure exists.

CLIP 3.3 Logan counts pennies
http://hein.pub/YCM3.3

As children learn the number words and the sequence, they also learn that *the counting sequence is fixed*: it remains the same all of the time (see Figure 3.1). When asked to count a set of bottle tops, Marvin counts "1, 2, 3, 4." And every time he is asked

Learning the Number Sequence

Note: These do not develop in any particular order.

Child's Understanding	Example (counting a collection of toy dinosaurs)
Knows some number words, not the sequence	1, 5, 3, 4, 3, 1
Knows some number words and partial sequence, not fixed sequence	*First count:* 1, 2, 3, 7, 5, 4 *Second count:* 1, 2, 3, 5, 8, 7
Knows number words and partial sequence, fixed sequence	*First count:* 1, 2, 3, 4, 5, 7, 9 *Second count:* 1, 2, 3, 4, 5, 7, 9
Knows number words, sequence, and sequence is fixed at least to 6	*First count:* 1, 2, 3, 4, 5, 6 *Second count:* 1, 2, 3, 4, 5, 6
Knows that later numbers in the sequence are formed by repeating aspects of the previously used sequence	1, 2, 3, 4, 5, 6, 7, 8, 9, 10, 8, 9, 10, 8

Figure 3.1 Learning the number sequence

to count, he uses the same sequence. A child may show that they understand that the sequence is fixed and not yet know the correct sequence. When Claudia counts 4 bottle tops, she consistently says, "1, 2, 4, 5." While she does not yet have the sequence correct (she skips 3), she does show that she knows the sequence is the same each time.

Supporting Development of the Counting Sequence

Supporting the development of the counting sequence involves time and experience counting. Varying the opportunities for counting can support participation and learning. Counting together with other students can provide supports for those who do not yet know the counting sequence. Counting through song and movement adds rhythm that can support students to keep track of the numbers and to recognize the pattern in the number sequence. Counting objects can also support students to learn the counting sequence. We have found in our research that many students can correctly count farther in the sequence when they are counting a collection of objects than they can when asked only to count out loud as far as they can.

Learning the One-to-One Principle

During a preschool experience visit designed for families at the town library, a mom sat with her two-and-a-half-year-old daughter Jennifer and her four-year-old son Jamie in front of a pile of small colored craft pom poms. Jamie lined up the pom poms, carefully saying, "1, 2, 3, 4, 5, 6, 7," one at a time as he put each pom pom into the line. Jamie was careful to count each pom pom exactly once and went back to the beginning to recount if he thought he had counted one twice or skipped one.

Jennifer moved the pom poms all over the table. Her mom leaned over and handed Jennifer a bag, asking her to put her pom poms away. One at a time, Jennifer put each pom pom in the bag then dumped them out and started again. She repeated this process five more times.

Though Jennifer and Jamie did different things with their pom poms, these two children were each working on aspects of one-to-one correspondence (the one-to-one principle). Jamie's understanding of the one-to-one principle is more readily evident, saying one number word for each object he counted. He even recounted over and over until he thought he had counted each object once. Jennifer was just beginning to deal with objects one at a time, which is a critical feature of using the one-to-one principle. She put each object one at a time into her bag. Continuing to develop her one-to-one correspondence will involve coordinating each object with a number word.

Just as with learning the counting sequence, developing understanding of one-to-one correspondence is not all or nothing. Children do not go from no

CLIP 3.4 James counts 8 bears
http://hein.pub/YCM3.4

CLIP 3.5 Lily counts 15 bears, then 6
http://hein.pub/YCM3.5

CLIP 3.6 Milani counts 24 caps
http://hein.pub/YCM3.6

understanding of one-to-one correspondence to complete understanding in a moment, or in a class day. And even when we think children have an understanding, we can see them developing a deeper understanding of this principle. Jennifer, above, shows early development of one-to-one correspondence, and we see a number of other ways in which children show partial understandings as they develop their one-to-one correspondence: some display one-to-one correspondence for only a part of the collection, some organize to support one-to-one correspondence while others do not, and some show one-to-one correspondence when counting some kinds of objects but not others, or in some situations but not in others. The following examples illustrate children's development of one-to-one correspondence.

Some Common Situations

Bernadette counts a collection of 12 markers (Figure 3.2). She points to a marker, saying "1," and points to another marker, saying "2." Then she points to two other markers and says "3."

She continues to count and recount the markers, but she is inconsistent in saying one number word for each marker (sometimes she counts two markers and says one number word and sometimes she skips a marker). Bernadette recognizes that her counting is not working well, so she decides to move each marker far across the floor as she counts it. She picks up a marker, says "1," and puts it down across the floor. She moves a second marker and says "2." She

Figure 3.2 Counting 12 markers

continues to move and count markers in this way. She correctly counts the first 5, saying one number word as she moves each marker.

Beyond the first 5 objects, Bernadette's one-to-one correspondence becomes inconsistent. As she moves the sixth marker across the floor she says two number words (*six, seven*) and intermittently does the same until she moves all 12 of her markers and her last number word is *fifteen*. Bernadette does not have perfect one-to-one correspondence, but she is developing the understanding that she needs to be careful with what she counts and that moving the objects as she counts can help her in this regard. As children develop one-to-one correspondence, we see that some show one-to-one correspondence at the beginning of their count but not for the entire count, and others show it at the beginning and the end but not in the middle, or vice versa. In other words, they demonstrate an emerging understanding of the one-to-one principle, even if they are inconsistent in being able to apply it accurately (Figure 3.3).

Camilo counts two different collections: a collection of 12 pennies and a collection of 17 colorful counting bears. He counts his 12 pennies by first spreading them out, then pointing at pennies and saying number words. But Camilo does not consistently assign one number word to each penny he touches—he sometimes says an additional number word as he transitions between touching pennies. A few moments later, however, Camilo correctly counts 17 bears. He carefully stands each bear up as he counts one number word for each bear. Here, Camilo demonstrates consistent one-to-one correspondence, which he did not do with the pennies.

CLIP 3.7 Mia counts and recounts 15 bears
http://hein.pub/YCM3.7

Camilo's counting illustrates how the materials children count can influence their use of the counting principles. Standing up the bears may have supported Camilo to move more carefully and more readily connect exactly one number word to each bear.

Supporting Development of One-to-One Correspondence

Developing one-to-one correspondence occurs as children work to coordinate the counting of each object with one and only one number word. You can support the development of one-to-one correspondence by counting together with children, emphasizing matching the action of pointing, touching, or moving each object with the saying of a single number word. Or you might pose a question to the student such as, "How will you keep track of which ones you've counted and which ones you haven't counted yet?" Some children benefit from putting the objects into a container as they count (such as during cleanup), as it slows down their count and focuses them on one object at a time. Other children find that spreading out their

Learning One-to-One Correspondence

Note: These do not develop in any particular order.

Child's Understanding	Example (counting a collection of 6 colored discs)
Move discs one at a time, no counting words	*Puts them one at a time on a plate*
Touches some discs and not the others, one number word for each	⬤ ⬤ ⬤ ⬤ ⬤ ⬤ 1 2 3 4 5
Touches each disc and at times says more than one number word	⬤ ⬤ ⬤ ⬤ ⬤ 1 2,3 4 5 6,7
Moves each disc one at a time, saying one word for the first few	⬤ ⬤ ⬤ ⬤ ⬤ ⬤ 1 2 3
Touches the discs in the pile, saying one number word for each disc at the beginning and the end but not in the middle	⬤ ⬤ ⬤ ⬤ ⬤ ⬤ 1 2 3,4 5 6,7 8
One number word for each object with bears but not discs	
One number word for each object counted	⬤ ⬤ ⬤ ⬤ ⬤ ⬤ 1 2 3 4 5 6

CLIP 3.8 Example of child who touches each object without saying number words http://hein.pub/YCM3.8

CLIP 3.9 Example of child who counts some objects more than once http://hein.pub/YCM3.9

CLIP 3.10 Example of child who counts without touching objects http://hein.pub/YCM3.10

CLIP 3.11 Example of child who skips an object http://hein.pub/YCM3.11

CLIP 3.12 Example of child with accurate one-to-one correspondence http://hein.pub/YCM3.12

Figure 3.3 Developing one-to-one correspondence

collection or working with a partner is helpful. However, supporting children to use strategies to keep track of the objects counted will not immediately move children to use the one-to-one principle. Developing understanding of and the ability to use the one-to-one principle takes time and a range of experiences.

Learning the Cardinal Principle

Capturing a child's understanding of the cardinal principle while they are counting can be challenging, as children don't necessarily end the process of counting by explicitly stating the total amount that they have in their collection. A child may know that counting objects involves reciting a sequence of numbers, but not that the outcome of this process is a number that represents the total quantity. For example, a child may say "1, 2, 3, 4" as they count a collection of 4, but this does not necessarily mean that the child understands that there is a quantity of 4 objects. Applying the cardinal principle requires that children name the set according to the last number used in their count. In this case, that last number used was 4, so there are 4 objects in the collection. Because the process of counting and what the count tells you are not necessarily the same thing, figuring out what a child knows about the cardinal principle often requires waiting for a child to complete their count and then asking a question like, "So, how many do you have in your collection?" Other ways to get at the cardinal principle could include saying to the child: "Here are some blocks. How many are there?" Or "Do you have enough to give me 4?" Asking children to make a set of objects of a given size rather than counting a given collection also can focus them on the cardinal principle.

CLIP 3.13 Fina counts 8 rocks
http://hein.pub/YCM3.13

CLIP 3.14 Leonardo counts bears
http://hein.pub/YCM3.14

When children who do not yet understand the cardinal principle are asked how many are in their collection, they often respond by counting again (see Figure 3.4). For example, Katie correctly counts 4 carrots, but when asked how many carrots she has, she counts them again "1, 2, 3, 4" and still cannot tell her teacher that there are 4 carrots. Other children who do not understand the cardinal principle may choose a seemingly random number when asked how many are in their collection.

Learning the Cardinal Principle

Note: These do not develop in any particular order.

Child's Understanding	Example (counting a collection of 11 pennies, then answering the question "How many pennies are in your collection?")
States a random number; does not name the last number stated when counting	Counts the collection and last number word is 6. Responds, "4."
Uses a nonnumber word to respond	Counts the collection and responds, "lots."
Never states how many in collection, only counts using number sequence and one-to-one correspondence	Recounts the collection again, last number word is 11. Counts and recounts but never says 11 in collection.
Uses the cardinal principle and states the last number counted, but count is incorrect due to an error in the counting sequence or one-to-one	Counts the collection and last number said is 9. Responds, "9."
Uses the cardinal principle and states last number counted, and count is correct	Counts the collection and last number said is 11. Responds, "11."

Figure 3.4 Children's development of the cardinal principle

After counting 4 carrots, for instance, they might say, "8!" Other children may tell the teacher they don't know how many there are in the collection, or they might say there are "a lot."

Supporting Development of the Cardinal Principle

Supporting children to make sense of the cardinal principle occurs as teachers follow up on children's counting by asking how many they have in their collection. You can provide additional support by checking the quantity with the student. When you ask how many, and the student is not sure, you can say: "Let's see, are there 4? Let's check together." You can also support cardinality when you gesture over the entire collection while restating the final number (indicating that the final number counted tells the amount in the collection) or when you work with small collections, where students can easily count and see the quantity.

Learning to Organize the Count and Count the Entire Collection

A feature of children's work as they count a collection of objects, and particularly as they make sure they are counting the entire collection, is how they organize their collection for counting. Organizing their collection provides support for children as they manage counting their entire collection. Organizing a collection can also support children as they develop and use the counting principles (Figure 3.5).

Children have a variety of legitimate ways of organizing, though they may not match an adult's ideas of organization. Often our expectation is that children will line up their objects first, then move down the line, touching each object with each counting word. Certainly many children will, at some point, line up the objects in their collection. However, they rarely start counting collections this way. Rather, children may count their objects in a pile, moving from object to object. Often their movement and counting may seem unsystematic to us; however, the child may have a system for making sure that each item is counted that we cannot yet see. The important idea is that a child's organizational scheme works for and makes sense to the child.

Figure 3.5 Organizing cars to count them

When children lay out their collection in an ordered way, it can support them to ensure that they have counted their entire collection. If a child organizes their collection by spreading out the objects, making piles, moving them as they count, lining them up, and so on, the child can more readily see what has and has not been counted. When children sort the objects by an attribute of the collection (color, size, type), it can give them a way to count more of the collection (Figure 3.6). For instance, a child who may only be able to count to 5 might only try to count part of a collection of 12 wooden blocks. However, when counting 12 colored pom poms, the child can first sort by color and count the 3 red ones, 3 blue ones, 3 white ones, and 3 yellow ones with "1, 2, 3." Thus, the child may work through counting the entire collection and work on one-to-one correspondence (counting 1, 2, 3 with each set of pom poms) and cardinality (how many red ones?).

CLIP 3.15 Example of child who does not count the entire collection http://hein.pub/YCM3.15

Figure 3.6 Sorting objects by attributes before counting

Although we may be tempted to encourage children to use particular organizational strategies to count objects, such as lining them up, this is not initially apparent or easy. Children need to understand the goal of organizing; otherwise, for example, lining up objects becomes an end in itself and may or may not support the child to count more accurately. We have seen children count 8 bears already lined up but not get an accurate count (e.g., their one-to-one correspondence is inconsistent as they move their pointing finger quickly across the row of bears). Yet these same children counted a pile of 15 bears that they organized correctly themselves (e.g., standing up each bear while counting carefully). Working with organization takes time to develop and is often an individualized experience for each child.

CLIP 3.16 Gracie counts 8 organized and then 8 unorganized bears http://hein.pub/YCM3.16

Supporting Development of Organization

Supporting children's development of organization as they count their collections occurs as we allow children to organize their collections in ways that make sense to them. You can ask children how they organized their collection, ask them if there is another way to organize their collection, share different ways that other children

CLIP 3.17 Joshua counts and sorts 15 airplanes
http://hein.pub/YCM3.17

CLIP 3.18 Christian makes a set of 27 blocks
http://hein.pub/YCM3.18

have organized their collections, provide different collections of objects that would encourage children to lay them out in a particular way, or provide organizational tools such as mats or counting strips. What is important to remember is that organizing a count is part of the sense making children are engaged in while counting and asking children to organize in a particular way may not make sense to them.

Teacher Reflections

Our eyes are trained to see if they get the right answer, then they are right and if they don't get the right answer, we are failing too. Versus now I can see he is building all these skills and he might not know rote counting but he can do this, that, and the other. That's been the most powerful . . . It opened up my eyes that they are all making some progress. Before I was very frustrated by that one child who couldn't count by rote. I wasn't even aware of the one-to-one. Maybe they could do it, but I wasn't looking for it.

—**Natali Gaxiola,** *preschool teacher*

This rocked our world. Especially the idea that they didn't have to have rote memorization to go beyond that. We were hung up on that. We used to use that as a milestone. Now we are looking for a pattern or rhythm and letting them go beyond 10. Way different this year.

—**Dorie Meek,** *preschool teacher*

Concurrent Development

The counting principles develop concurrently and in relation to children's experiences and existing understandings. The counting principles do not develop in a set order or in the same ways for all children. This means that not all children will learn the counting sequence before understanding one-to-one correspondence or understand one-to-one correspondence before developing the cardinal principle. However, we do see that each and every child comes to preschool with some knowledge and understanding of counting. Finding out what children know requires first attending to each child and the range of counting principles and partial understandings the child demonstrates. This allows us to know if what we are asking makes sense to the child, and if the collection is one that supports his use of counting.

The following scenarios offer a few examples of how the counting principles may develop in relation to each other. These examples are not intended to be exhaustive but to provide insight into the details of what to look for as children develop their understanding of counting. Each scenario provides a potential set of understandings of one child.

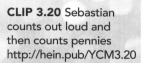
CLIP 3.19 Bryan counts 15 bears
http://hein.pub/YCM3.19

CLIP 3.20 Sebastian counts out loud and then counts pennies
http://hein.pub/YCM3.20

Devon's Understanding of Counting

Little knowledge of the counting sequence

Little understanding of the one-to-one principle

No understanding of the cardinal principle

As Devon tries to count 6 toy animals (see Figure 3.7), he touches the brontosaurus and says, "3," the triceratops and says, "2, 1, 5," the dimetrodon and says, "3," the mammoth and says, "1, 3." When asked how many animals in his collection, he begins to count again.

Devon knows that counting the collection involves saying number words and touching the objects. He does not yet know the beginning of the counting sequence, that you

Figure 3.7 Devon's 6 dinosaurs

only say a number once, or the correct count sequence. He does *not* say one counting word for each object he touches (one-to-one correspondence), and when asked how many animals he had, he started counting over again (the cardinal principle). Devon demonstrates little knowledge of the counting sequence, little understanding of the one-to-one correspondence, and no understanding of the cardinal principle.

Chelo's Understanding of Counting

Limited knowledge of the counting sequence

No understanding of the cardinal principle

Correct use of one-to-one correspondence

In counting her 8 bears, Chelo touched each bear one at a time and assigned one number word to each bear: "1, 2, 2, 5, 9, 2, 5, 9." When asked how many bears she has she responds "2."

Chelo knows how to start the counting sequence and she knows some of the number names. She does not yet know the counting sequence up to 8 or that the numbers in the sequence do not repeat. She knows something about one-to-one correspondence, pointing to each bear and saying one number word, even though the numbers are not in sequence. She does not show that she understands the cardinal principle. When asked "How many?" she answers "2," which is not the last number she said when counting the collection.

Hector's Understanding of Counting

Knows the counting sequence

Is able to apply the cardinal principle

Little understanding of one-to-one correspondence

Hector counts his pile of 8 bears by lining them up first without saying any numbers. The bears are close together. He then counts more quickly than his finger moves to point to each bear, saying, "1, 2, 3, 4, 5, 6, 7, 8, 9, 10, 11." When asked how many bears he has, Hector says he has 11 bears.

Eleven was the last number Hector said, not because he does not know the counting sequence, but because he touched one bear and said more than one number (in touching the yellow bear, for instance, he said, "3, 4"). Hector knows the counting sequence to 11. He knows that the last number in the count represents the total number in his collection (the cardinal principle). But he does not clearly understand one-to-one correspondence. Interestingly, he lined up the bears, but he does not yet use his lining up to correctly employ one-to-one correspondence.

Noemi's Understanding of Counting

Knows the counting sequence at least as far as 8

Understands the cardinal principle

Understands one-to-one correspondence

Noemi is asked to grab a set of 8 bears from a larger bin of counting bears. She begins taking 1 bear out at a time, counting one number for each bear: "1, 2, 3, 4, 5, 6, 7, 8." Noemi stops when she has created a group of 8 bears. When asked how many bears are in her collection, she responds, "I have 8." Noemi is demonstrating understanding of the counting principles: the counting sequence (up to 8), the cardinal principle (responding to "how many" with the last number word she counted), and one-to-one correspondence (counting exactly one number for each bear).

Variability in Learning Counting Principles

These examples demonstrate that the counting principles do not develop in a set sequence. Some children learn a string of numbers in the counting sequence before they can apply this knowledge to count collections of objects. Other children develop some understanding of one-to-one correspondence before they learn much of the counting sequence. Children can correctly apply the cardinal principle and not yet have much understanding of one-to-one correspondence (or even the counting sequence). It is also the case that children work on learning these principles at the same time. As students work on one-to-one correspondence, they can further develop their knowledge of the counting sequence and the cardinal principle. As students work on counting the entire collection, they are working on the cardinal principle and so on. Working on the counting principles together supports learning and builds on the mathematical knowledge that children do have.

Supporting the Development of Counting

Seeing how children develop counting principles in different ways has significant implications for instruction. First, we can ask all children to count collections even if they don't yet know the counting sequence. Second, observing a child's counting and asking questions about what the child did can provide important insights. Third, there are benefits to counting collections greater than 5, 10, or even 20. Finally, the materials we ask children to count may influence their counting.

These key implications lead to other important ideas and strategies to remember as you support children learning to count.

You don't have to wait to have children count collections until they are proficient at reciting the counting sequence.
Children develop understanding of counting as they count collections because counting a collection gives them an opportunity to use each of the counting principles. We saw with Chelo that students can count a collection without knowing the

counting sequence and still productively be learning one-to-one correspondence, the cardinal principle and to count the entire set. Counting a collection can also create a need for the child to extend their counting sequence beyond where they may be comfortable. While we may hesitate to ask children to count collections when they do not yet have the correct number sequence because we are worried they are using the "wrong" numbers, we see these invented sequences as productive and a normal part of learning. Counting collections does not hamper children's use or learning of the counting sequence; rather, it is *through* counting the objects that children continue to build their understanding of the number sequence while coordinating the sequence with the other counting principles. We have also seen that children who do not know much about counting can benefit from counting a collection. They develop their understanding of the principles as they try to use them to count a collection.

Observe and ask questions.

It is striking how little we know about children's understanding of counting by just hearing the answer to "How many are there?" A child may respond "8" to a collection of 8 bears, but you need to know *how* the child got 8. Finding out what children know about counting requires watching and listening as they count, touch, organize and reorganize, stop and start, and complete their count. It may also require asking them, "I can see you counted your collection. Can you count it again so I can watch and listen?" In counting again not only do you get a chance to see specifically what the child is doing and saying, but the child also gets a chance to work through it again. Our challenge as teachers is to take a moment to observe and listen and not intervene too soon; we are often very quick to count with a student who doesn't yet know the sequence, or touch and point to each object for the student. We need to let children work through counting their collections, and listen and watch, before we help them.

It can be productive to have children count larger collections.

Our research shows benefits to counting larger collections. Larger collections would be ones that go beyond our typical expectations and often beyond what we think children know about counting. School mathematics often sequences the range of children's counting: counting to 3 then to 4 and then to 5, counting 10, and so on. Asking children to count larger collections creates space for them to work on acquiring the principles and gives the teacher a chance to see a broader picture of what the child knows about counting. Given what we have seen in the development of the counting principles, it makes sense that children could work on counting a collection that extends their counting sequence. In our experience, children often know later parts of the sequence even if they don't know all of the earlier parts. In a recent study, 70 percent of preschool students who did not show evidence of one-to-one correspondence when counting a set of 8 bears did show some evidence of one-to-one correspondence when counting a collection of 31 pennies. In addition, 40 percent of the students we assessed counted higher in the number sequence when counting the 31 pennies than when we asked them to count orally as high as they could without objects.

Have children count different materials.

Earlier in the chapter we pointed out how counting different materials (pennies versus bears, for example) can influence a child's use of the counting principles. So, if a child seems to be struggling to count a collection, it might help to consider a different type of object to count. For example, a preschool teacher was concerned that one of her students was struggling with counting and did not know the counting sequence beyond 5. During a home visit she learned that the family placed very high value on science and that the child was particularly knowledgeable about marine animals. The day after the home visit, the teacher noticed the child looking at a stuffed shark on the floor. When she asked him how many teeth his shark had, he correctly counted (using all of the counting principles) to 13. This example helps us see that what children count matters and also that what we see a child do at school may not capture all of what the child knows and understands. We need to use a range of approaches to create opportunities for children to display their competencies.

We provide more ideas about supporting children's counting in Chapters 5 and 7. First, though, we examine how children can build on their understanding of counting collections to solve problems.

Questions for Further Reflection

1. As you observe students on the playground or in free play, look for an opportunity to watch or ask them to count. Watch and listen to see which of the counting principles they demonstrate.

2. Invite a child you know to count out loud as far as they can. Then ask them to count a collection of objects. What do you notice about their use of the counting sequence?

3. Invite a child you know to count two collections of objects of similar amounts. For one collection, line up the objects for the child and then ask them to count. For the other collection, present the collection unorganized and ask the child to count. How did the child count in the different situations?

4. Invite a child you know to count a collection of 8 objects, a collection of 15 objects, and a collection of 31 objects. What do you notice about their use of the counting principles?

5. Watch Hazel count 30 pennies in clip 3.21. What do you notice? Watch a second time. What do you notice the second time that you didn't see the first time? What does Hazel show she understands about (1) the sequence of number names, (2) the one-to-one principle, and (3) the cardinal principle?

CLIP 3.21 Hazel counts 30 pennies
http://hein.pub/YCM3.21

6. Consider that you have a student who can use one-to-one correspondence with confidence to count a collection of 23 objects, but the student continues to struggle with the counting sequence, most often skipping some of the teens. How might you support the student?

7. Watch Gracie count 31 pennies in clip 3.22. What do you notice about her counting? What could you ask her next about her pennies that she just counted?

CLIP 3.22 Gracie counts 31 pennies
http://hein.pub/YCM3.22

4

Extending Counting to Solve Problems

Young children can apply their emerging counting skills to solve a variety of problems that arise as they are developing understanding of and skill in counting. In addition to providing variety and interest to counting collections, using counting to solve problems calls attention to counting principles, requires children to be flexible in counting, and shows that counting is a tool that can be used to solve problems.

In this chapter, we provide a snapshot of the overarching principles that help us understand how children think about and solve different problems. In particular, we classify different types of problems that children can solve as they are learning to count, describe the strategies that children typically use to solve specific types of problems, and show how these strategies evolve with the development of children's counting.

Extending Counting

When counting a collection, a number of scenarios can arise that engage students in thinking about joining, separating, comparing, and grouping the items in their collections. This can happen informally as children notice things about their collection or as you ask questions about it.

For example: This day Yaya and the rest of the children are sorting buttons for the button store they decided to create in the dramatic play area of the classroom. They are sorting the buttons into piles of different sizes and types so they can price them. Yaya is making a pile of red buttons on the table in front of her. When Mr. McMillan comes to the table where Yaya is working, she has made a pile of 7 red buttons.

Mr. M sits down and asks Yaya what she is doing.

Yaya: *I'm getting red buttons.*

Mr. M: *Yaya, how many buttons do you have in your pile right now?*

Yaya: [with no hesitation, counts the buttons in the pile she has made] *1, 2, 3, 4, 5, 6, 7* [looking up at Mr. McMillan] *7.*

Mr. M: *If you put 2 more buttons with the 7 you have there, how many would you have then?*

Yaya: [adds 2 more red buttons to her pile and then counts the 9 buttons now in her pile] *1, 2, 3, 4, 5, 6, 7, 8, 9* [with emphasis on the 9].

Mr. M: *So how many buttons do you have now?*

Yaya: *9.*

Mr. M: *Okay. Now suppose someone came to your button store and bought 3 of your red buttons. How many red buttons would you have left?*

Yaya: [removes 3 buttons from her pile of 9 buttons and counts the remaining buttons] *1, 2, 3, 4, 5, 6. I have 6.*

Mr. M: *Good. Now I want to know how many buttons you would have to put with those 6 buttons to have 8 buttons altogether?*

Yaya: [adds 1 red button to her collection of buttons, then counts the buttons in the collection] *1, 2, 3, 4, 5, 6, 7.*

[She recognizes that she does not have enough buttons, so she adds another button to her pile. Again she counts all the buttons, starting with the original 6.]

Yaya: *1, 2, 3, 4, 5, 6, 7, 8.*

[She has kept the 2 buttons she added separate from the other 6. She looks at them.]

Yaya: *I needed 2 more.*

For all three problems, Yaya carried out the action with the buttons that was posed in the problem. She added buttons to her collection or took buttons away, depending on the question posed. These examples illustrate how children can solve a variety of problems as they are developing their understanding of counting. Children develop ways to use the objects in their collection to solve problems in ways that lay the foundation for using modeling and counting to solve more abstract arithmetic problems. In the following sections, we describe the strategies that children use for a variety of types of problems.

A Range of Problems and Strategies

As illustrated by Yaya's solutions to the three problems Mr. McMillan posed, young children consistently use strategies that reflect the action or relationships described in the problem that they are trying to solve. The situations most often encountered by young children are those that ask them to join, to separate, to compare, or to create groups.

Joining

Consider how the following joining situation, in which objects are added to the collection, emerges and the range of strategies children can use to solve it.

Ms. Moulton sat with a small group of her kindergarteners as they were counting collections with a partner. Stephan and Geraldine were counting a collection of baseball cards. They had laid out their 8 cards all over the table and counted them, touching each card together. Ms. Moulton decided to ask them a few questions about their collection.

Ms. M: *I see you have counted your collection. How many baseball cards do you have in your collection?*

Stephan: *8.*

Ms. M: *8. Geraldine, do you agree?*

[Geraldine nods yes.]

Ms. M: *Okay. I found 3 more baseball cards. Would you like to add these to your collection?*

Stephan and Geraldine: *Yes!*

Ms. M: *So how many do you have in your collection so far?*

Stephan and Geraldine: *8.*

Ms. M: *So you have 8 baseball cards, and here are 3 more for your collec-tion* [hands Stephan 3 baseball cards]. *How many baseball cards do you have in your collection now?*

The children work on the problem as Ms. Moulton watches Stephan put the 3 new cards into his collection and count all of the baseball cards together. While Stephan is doing this work, Geraldine is doing something on her fingers. When they appear to be finished, Ms. Moulton asks Stephan what he was doing with the collection.

Ms. M: *Stephan, I noticed you were doing something with the collec-tion to find out how many you have now. Can you tell me what you were doing?*

Stephan: *I counted them.*

Ms. M: *Can you tell us how you counted them?*

Stephan: *I had the 8 and I pushed them together with the new ones and then I counted again.*

Ms. M: *Can you show us how you counted?*

Stephan: *1, 2, 3, 4, 5, 6, 7, 8, 9, 10, 11* [pointing to each baseball card as he counts it].

Ms. M: *Geraldine, did you see what Stephan did?*

[Geraldine nods yes.]

Ms. M: *I did not see you using all of the cards. Did you do it the same way, or a different way than Stephan? Stephan, let's see if we can see what Geraldine did.*

Geraldine: *I remembered that we had 8 baseball cards in our collection. So I only counted the new ones.*

Ms. M: *Can you show us?*

Geraldine: *I counted like, 8* [waves hand over original 8 baseball cards and pauses], . . . *9* [touches 1 of the new cards], *10* [touches another new card], *11* [touches the last new card].

Ms. M: *So it looks like you both found out how many cards in your new collection.*

Geraldine: [smiles] *Yep.*

Ms. M: *So the two of you, how many are in your collection of baseball cards now?*

Stephan and Geraldine: *11.*

Ms. M: *Is your new collection larger or smaller than the collection you started with?*

Stephan and Geraldine: *Bigger.*

Stephan followed the action in the situation that Ms. Moulton created. He took his initial collection of 8 cards and then joined the 3 new cards with those cards and counted all the cards. Geraldine was able to use the fact that she had already counted the collection and understood that there were 8, so she did not have to recount those cards and could start counting on from 8. Geraldine's strategy required that she could start counting at a number greater than 1, an understanding that many children are still developing at age five; it also required that she recognize that this understanding could be used in counting objects, and that she could use it to figure out the number in her collection when more were joined to the original collection.

A Different Type of Joining Problem

Sometimes when counting a collection the child wants to find out how many more they need to have a certain amount: I have 7 box tops, how many more will I need to get to have 10? This situation is like the first joining problem in that it involves adding objects to a collection, but the unknown (what the child is asked to figure out) is different. In this case the unknown is the number of objects that need to be added to a collection to get a given total. In this example, Ms. Moulton is talking with Annie, who has been counting clothespins.

> **Ms. M:** *So Annie you said you have 15 clothespins in your collection. How many more clothespins would you need to get out of the clothespin bag* [holds up the bag of clothespins] *so that you would have 17 in your collection?*
>
> **Annie:** *Hmm* [counts her collection again]. *1, 2, 3, 4 . . . 15* [reaches for the bag and takes out 1 and adds it the pile and counts again from 1], *1, 2, 3, 4 . . . 16* [reaches for the bag and takes out 1, adds it to the pile and counts again], *1, 2, 3, 4, . . . 17.*
>
> **Ms. M:** *So how many more did you need to add so that you have 17?*
>
> **Annie:** *2* [touches the 2 from the bag] *1, 2.*

Annie solved the problem by first adding 1 clothespin and then recounting the collection. When she found she did not have 17 clothespins, she added 1 more, and again counted the whole collection. When she found that she now had 17 clothespins, the teacher prompted her about how many she added to her collection and she counted the 2 clothespins she had added.

Some children will start solving the problem the same way that Annie did, but might not know to keep the clothespins they add separate from the set of 15 that were there to start with. So when they are done adding more clothespins, they cannot figure out how many clothespins they added. Often when this happens the child responds with the new total in the collection, in this case 17, as their answer.

Other children make use of the knowledge that there are 15 clothespins in the initial pile, so they do not have to recount them. Instead they start counting on from 15 as they add clothespins, adding 1 clothespin and saying "16," then adding a second clothespin and saying "17." Then, looking at the 2 clothespins they added, they can respond that they needed 2 more. This strategy is similar to what Geraldine had done earlier, counting on from the 8 baseball cards rather than recounting all of them starting at 1.

Separating

Another common situation that can arise when counting a collection is when items are removed or separated from a given collection. Ms. Moulton returns to Annie, who has now counted out a collection of 18 colored clothespins. Ms. Moulton poses a problem that involves removing clothespins from the collection Annie has created.

CLIP 4.1 Errington counts and separates airplanes
http://hein.pub/YCM4.1

CLIP 4.2 Sofia counts and separates bears
http://hein.pub/YCM4.2

CLIP 4.3 Gracie counts, recounts, then separates bears
http://hein.pub/YCM4.3

> **Ms. M:** *Annie, how many clothespins do you have in your collection?*
>
> **Annie:** *18. I have 6 blue ones, 4 green ones, 5 red ones, and 3 yellow ones.*
>
> **Ms. M:** *Let's take out one color and see how many you have left.*
>
> **Annie:** *Let's take the yellow ones.*
>
> **Ms. M:** *Okay. So you had 18 and you take away 3 yellow ones. How many clothespins do you have now?*
>
> **Annie:** [removes 3 yellow clothespins from the group of 18 clothespins and counts the remaining clothespins by ones] *15. I have 15 left.*

Annie solved this problem by following the action in the situation. She separated out the yellow clothespins from the entire collection and then counted how many clothespins still remained.

Comparing Two Groups

Counting collections readily creates opportunities for children to compare. They can compare the attributes of objects in their collection (do I have more red or purple crayons?), or they can compare their collection to another child's collection. Sometimes children want to find out who has more; other times they want to know how many more. Children can often decide which group is larger by counting the two groups. The number that comes later in the counting sequence represents the larger group. For example, a child might say that 15 is more than 12 because 15 comes after 12. Finding how much bigger the larger group is turns out to be more complicated.

One strategy children can use to answer this question is to match objects in the smaller group with objects in the larger group until the objects in the smaller group are used up. Counting the unmatched objects in the larger group tells how many more objects there are in the larger group than in the smaller group. This strategy is illustrated in the following example.

In this example, Ike had carried a bin with animals over to the math table. He had a piece of construction paper folded in half and explained to Ms. Sanchez that the small animals lived on one side of the paper and the big animals lived on the other. He took animals out of the bin one at a time, making a different sound for each as he placed them in their homes.

Ms. S: *How many big animals do you have?*

Ike: [pointing to each animal as he counts] *1, 2, 3, 4, 5, 6, 7.*

Ms. S: *Ah, and how many small animals do you have?*

Ike: [pointing to each animal] *1, 2, 3, 4, 5—I have 5 small ones.*

Ms. S: *Interesting. So do you have more big animals or more small animals?*

Ike: *More big ones.*

Ms. S: *How many more big animals are there?*

Ike: [lining the animals up nose to nose on either side of the folded line while keeping them each on their side] *There's 2 more big ones. See!*

CLIP 4.4 Christian counts and compares bears
http://hein.pub/YCM4.4

Counting and Constructing Equal Groups

Another type of situation that arises when children are counting involves placing objects into equal groups. For example, during choice time, four children are playing with the blocks and the cars making a garage. They park 3 cars in each space. Ms. Valentine stops by and asks them how many cars they have in each space. They tell her they have 3. She asks them how many parking spaces there are and they answer 4. She then follows that up with, "Wow, so if you have 3 cars in each of your parking spaces, and there are 4 parking spaces, how many cars do you have parked in your garage?" Most children count all the cars in the parking spaces starting with 1 and counting to 12, but one child uses the knowledge that there are 3 cars in each parking space and counts on from the 3 in the first space, saying, "4, 5, 6, 7, 8, 9, 10, 11, 12." Another child knows that 3 + 3 = 6, and starts counting the remaining cars starting with 7.

Children can also solve problems in which the goal is to construct equal groups from a given collection. In one situation children construct equal groups of a given size and count the number of groups they make; in the other children share the objects equally between a given number of groups and find the number of objects in each group. In the first situation, the children may have 12 cars and want to put 3 cars in each space, so they have to figure out how many parking spaces they will need to make. In the second situation, the children have 12 cars and they know they have 4 spaces, so they have to figure out how many cars they can put in each space if there are the same number of cars in each space.

Children solve the first type of problem by making groups of the given size and counting the groups they have made. For example, they would take their 12 cars and put them in groups of 3 (essentially put them in their parking spaces) until all 12 cars are in their spaces. They would count the groups of 3 they made (how many parking spaces). In the second situation, the children would take their 12 cars, make their 4 parking spaces, and then pass out their 12 cars one at a time to each of the parking spaces until they had passed out all of their cars. They could then count the number of cars in one of the parking spaces to find their answer.

CLIP 4.5 Aileen counts ears on bears
http://hein.pub/YCM4.5

CLIP 4.6 Hector shares crayons
http://hein.pub/YCM4.6

Conclusion

Our purpose in describing strategies that children use to solve problems is not to provide examples of strategies to be shown to children for them to imitate. Children employ these strategies naturally, and any attempt to demonstrate these strategies and have children practice them would be counterproductive. We need to trust children's intuitive ability to use their emerging counting skills to represent problems. Young children know a lot more about fundamental ideas underlying arithmetic than we typically have given them credit for. We want to support children to build upon and extend their informal strategies both to develop understanding for arithmetic that is consistent with the ways they naturally think about arithmetic operations and to foster the continued development of their problem solving.

In the problems posed in this chapter, the students start with a collection or collections of objects they have constructed. The problems the children are asked to solve are posed after the initial collection is counted out; they are about collections the children have already made. There are advantages to having the children solve problems that emerge out of a collection they have already counted. When the children have counted the collection, they have developed a context for understanding of the quantity in the collection. They essentially understand the context in which the problem is situated, and they have actually started to solve the problem by constructing the collection that is its starting place. What is left is to figure out what to do to that collection (add objects to it, take objects from it, group the objects in some way). Because children naturally model the actions and relationships involved in these situations, they can begin to solve problems in ways that do not require a formal understanding of the operations of addition, subtraction, multiplication, and division.

It is tempting to wait until children have become proficient at all of the counting principles before attempting to pose problems. However, robust learning happens when posing problems regardless of whether the student has accurately counted the initial collection. When problems are posed, children are provided more opportunities to count and re-count their collection. They are asked to make their collections larger, to make their collections smaller, to consider different portions of their collection. All of these opportunities support students to work on their understanding of the counting principles; in this way, children continue to learn to count in the context of solving problems.

Teacher Reflection

Counting collections helps me better prepare my students for the work of problem solving. During counting collections, students work with objects and tools (such as ten-frames, hundreds charts, and number lines) as they count. This familiarity with classroom math tools helps them to use objects (such as Unifix cubes) in their problem-solving work. Asking students to record how they have counted their collection helps to prepare them to record their thinking during problem solving.

—**Trish Morrissey,** *kindergarten teacher*

In Chapter 6, we discuss problems for which children must also construct the initial collection as part of the problem-solving process. In those problems information about the initial set and the operations on it are often presented at the same time. But before we consider these more complex problems, we describe in Chapter 5 a variety of classroom spaces in which problems and situations like the ones we have discussed in this chapter and in Chapter 3 occur.

Questions for Further Reflection

1. Take the problems described in this chapter and for each problem make up a similar type of problem with a different context that might be appropriate for children in your class.

2. How do you think different children in your class might respond to these problems?

3. Try the problems with your class or with some children in your class. How did the children solve the problems you posed?

4. Which types of problems do you find most appropriate for children in your class? Why?

5. As you observe students in free play, look for an opportunity where they are counting and ask a follow-up question that would require them to join more or separate some from the group they counted. Watch to see how they solve the problem you posed.

6. Watch video clip 4.7, which takes place after Christian has already counted 15 bears. What do you notice about his strategy? If you were the interviewer, what would be your next move?

CLIP 4.7 Christian counts and joins bears
http://hein.pub/YCM4.7

Reference

Carpenter, T. P., E. Fennema, M. L. Franke, S. B. Empson, and L. W. Levi. 2015. *Children's Mathematics: Cognitively Guided Instruction*. 2nd ed. Portsmouth, NH: Heinemann.

5

Classroom Spaces That Support Children's Counting

Teachers in an early childhood setting have the unique opportunity to incorporate math skills into every area of their children's day. To do so effectively, they must be conscious and aware of the best ways to utilize those skills and differentiate their activities so that every child has the ability to engage with mathematical learning.

—Heidi Schultz, prekindergarten teacher

Math is everywhere and math opportunities are abundant in children's play. It's using all kinds of materials in a math way. Being purposeful about materials—and even then, allowing kids to show you how to use the materials in a math way that you never even thought of.

—Renae DeBarbieri, prekindergarten teacher

In the previous two chapters, we detailed the range of understandings children demonstrate as they learn to count and begin to solve problems. In this chapter, we discuss different spaces in the classroom in which these opportunities abound. We provide examples of ways in which teachers notice, support, and extend children's counting in various classroom spaces and show how young children's mathematical understandings can be enriched through the activities that they engage with, the questions they are asked, and the materials made available to them. The big ideas that will be discussed throughout the chapter are:

- Mathematics emerges in everyday activities.
- A range of mathematics can be worked on in different activities, and you can decide what you want to focus on.
- Different questions that you ask are going to take you in different directions.

To demonstrate the many places where children engage with mathematics, we have organized the chapter by "classroom spaces" that include routines and transitions, center activities, pretend contexts, and math-time activities. Although we refer to these as "classroom spaces," many of these contexts are available both in and out of school. Furthermore, we recognize the blurry lines between spaces and find it particularly important to attend to how children demonstrate their understanding across and between spaces. The examples we provide are intended as illustrations of the ways that we have observed teachers make use of children's thinking in their teaching, not as prescriptions for what teachers should do. There are, of course, many different ways that you might apply and adapt these ideas to your own contexts. We have found that an easy way to get started is simply to observe and listen closely to children as they count or start to solve problems. Providing opportunities for children to count objects, and noticing the details of how they do so, can help you see what a child knows and consider what else you want to learn about a child's mathematical ideas.

In the example below, several children are gathering leaves during outside playtime. After working for several minutes, they are eager to share their leaf collections with their teacher. Owen and Addy approach Ms. Mara, carrying their leaves in their hands.

Addy: *Look!*

Ms. M: *What do you have, Addy?*

Addy: *Leafs!*

Ms. M: *How many leaves do you have?*

Addy: [puts leaves down on the ground, one at a time, as she counts] *1, 2, 3, 4, 5. I have 5!* [flashes 5 fingers]

Ms. M: *How about you, Owen?*

Owen: [puts his 6 leaves down on the ground in a pile; some leaves are covering each other; counts quickly while pointing generally at the pile] *1, 2, 3, 4, 5, 6, 7, 8, 9, 10.*

Ms. M: *You have some leaves too!*

By noticing an opportunity to briefly mathematize their play, and by attending closely to how they counted, Ms. Mara was able to learn about Addy and Owen's counting. Specifically, she learned that Addy was able to accurately count a set of 5 leaves, applying the one-to-one and cardinal principles. Addy was also able to connect her count of 5 leaves to a representation of 5 fingers. Owen demonstrated that he knew the counting sequence to 10, but in this instance did not assign number names to individual leaves. Ms. Mara chose not to intervene further in this case; she was focused on learning about Owen and Addy's thinking. She knows that there will be many more opportunities to listen and observe Owen and Addy's counting that will help her to recognize what they know and inform her efforts to support and extend their learning.

Routines and Transitions

Teachers in the early childhood classrooms leverage and build from children's existing rich understanding about mathematics. As we spend time in preschool and kindergarten classrooms, we see this happening throughout the daily routines that teachers set up. Many teachers find that daily routines and transitions provide a variety of opportunities to purposefully orchestrate engagement with counting and number. And because these activities occur regularly, they can provide a space to observe and learn about children's thinking over time. There are many routines and transitions during the day where children can engage in counting or problem solving. We discuss four here—taking attendance, returning library books, lining up, and mealtime—but there are many others. We also have seen teachers engage children in counting and problem solving while getting ready to go home or outside or in transition between meals and the next activity.

CLIP 5.1 Birthday countdown
http://hein.pub/YCM5.1

Taking Attendance

We have seen many teachers organize attendance taking as a counting activity by having a child lead the class in counting the number of children present. This can be a good way to provide children with an opportunity to practice counting and for the teacher to listen and observe. We have also seen classrooms where teachers start the year off this way but then add some complexity to the routine.

In the following example, we see how Ms. Marley changed her routine for taking attendance. She started the year by having the children count aloud with her as she held a hand over each child's head. After a few weeks, she had the children take turns leading the counting. One day after a discussion of how warm it was outside, she heard the children talking about how many children were wearing shorts that day. This gave her the idea to change her attendance-taking routine so that she could learn more about how children were solving problems.

Ms. M: *How can we find out how many children are wearing shorts or not today?*

Children: *We can count them.*

Ms. M: *Okay. Mia, you help us count our friends wearing shorts.*

Mia: [stands up and walks around the circle touching each child wearing shorts on the top of the head and counting with the rest of the class] *1, 2, 3, 4, 5, 6, 7, 8, 9—it is 9 shorts.*

Ms. M: *I like how Mia held her hand over each person so everyone knew when to count. I am going to write that on the board, 9 shorts. Now, Eddy, you count the number of children who are not wearing shorts.*

Eddy: [stays in his seat in the circle and points to the children not wearing shorts] *1, 2, 3, 4, 5, 6, 7—there are 7 pants. See I told you there is more shorts than pants.*

Ms. M: *Is Eddy right, are there more shorts than pants?*

Class: *Yes!*

From this interaction, Ms. Marley was able to observe Mia and Eddy's counting and also support all the children to think about how they might start comparing sets. After this interaction, counting two sets became a daily activity, and Ms. Marley let children take turns picking two things to count. She supported them in brainstorming different things to compare: tie-up shoes or not, long sleeves or short, hair ties or not, and so on. This routine provided children with the opportunity to both compare and combine sets every day. Some days Ms. Marley explored both of these practices by posing questions about comparing ("How many more?" or "How many fewer?") and about combining ("How many altogether?").

Returning Library Books

Ms. Hechinger structures opportunities for children to work on counting through their weekly library book routine, in which she collects children's library books as they arrive in the morning. As she engages with each child, she leverages these few moments to work on counting ideas.

Ms. H: *Hello, Liliana! How many books did you bring today? Can we count them to check?*

Liliana: [counting as Ms. Hechinger takes books out of her bag one at a time] *1, 2, 3, 4, 5, 6.*

Ms. H: *How many books?*

Liliana: *Um . . .*

Ms. H: *Let's count them one more time together.*

Liliana and Ms. H: [counting together, Ms. Hechinger emphasizes the last number with tone and slower speed] *1, 2, 3, 4, 5, 6.*

Ms. H: *So how many books?*

Liliana: *6.*

Ms. H: *Nice work. Can you count them one more time for me?*

Liliana: *1, 2, 3, 4, 5, 6. There are 6!*

After Liliana happily went to the rug to find a new book, Ms. Hechinger moved on to interacting with the next child. She eventually engaged with each child individually, varying her interactions based on how children were counting their library books (taking books out of the bag slowly with Enrique to support one-to-one correspondence, counting and recounting with Ana to support her use of the counting sequence, among others).

Lining Up

Many times during the day children line up, either to go out for recess, move to a different classroom, get ready to leave, or wash hands. All of this lining up provides a wonderful space for counting. We have seen teachers use this opportunity in many ways. Some have the class count together as each child gets in line, some have each child say their "number" as they get in the line, some wait and count the children after they are all in the line. There is no right or wrong way to do this; what is important is that the children engage in the counting rather than watch their teacher do it.

Meals and Snacks

Snack and mealtime offer a natural opportunity to count and solve problems, especially problems about sharing. There are usually a given number of children and a given number of crackers, fruit slices, and so on to hand out. Ms. Silver often works on counting with her helpers during snack time.

> *Sadie was the snack helper at Table 1. Ms. S handed her a bag of 12 orange slices and told her that each child should get 3 slices. She watched as Sadie got out one plate at a time, placed 3 slices on each plate, and then put the plate in front of a chair. After the fourth plate, Sadie said, "We have 5 chairs here but only 4 people get oranges."*

There are several questions Ms. Silver could pose to Sadie following this exchange. She could ask her how many more orange slices they needed. Or, how many orange slices she had passed out. For the second question, it would be interesting to see how Sadie solved the problem. She would likely count all of the oranges on the plates, but Ms. Silver could encourage her to think about the groups of oranges by asking her how many plates, how many oranges on each plate, and how many oranges altogether.

As these examples suggest, adding a few explicit questions or prompts to existing routines can provide children with multiple opportunities to count and solve problems throughout their day. Teachers might choose to focus on children's counting or to pose questions that get children to think about the mathematical relationships within given situations as Ms. Marley does when she has children compare sets during attendance taking. The ideas presented here do not have to add time to the day and might provide ideas for highlighting the mathematics already present in other everyday activities.

Seeded Mathematical Spaces

The examples described in this section occurred as a result of teachers' intentional efforts to "seed" the classroom environment with specific tools, games, or objects that create opportunities for children to engage in mathematics. These seeded opportunities can involve activities or games that have been introduced to children and then made available to explore during choice time, or they may be activities that caregivers engage children with outside of school. In each case, the first step in thinking about how to support children's learning is to attend to the ways they are counting and perhaps how they are posing problems for themselves. In the examples that we present, these observations have allowed teachers to think about the questions they want to ask and how they might support the child to take the next step.

Seeding Choice Time Activities: Combining Key Trains

Ms. Corry has several boxes filled with different items that she places around her room. The children in her class are free to explore with the materials in the boxes during choice time. One day Michael was exploring a box with keys, lining them up to make a train. Ms. Corry seizes the opportunity to ask Michael about counting and sets up a math problem by joining in the child's play.

Ms. C: *How long is your key train?*

Michael: [pointing to each key and quickly counting] *1, 2, 3, 4, 5, 6, 7, 8, 9, 10* [then slowly], *13, 15. It is 15 cars.*

Ms. C: *Wow, that is a long train!* [building her own train with 5 more keys] *My train is short. How long will your train be if all the cars on my train move to yours?*

Michael: [counting each key again] *1, 2, 3, 4, 5, 6, 7, 8, 9, 10, 13, 15* [then moving the keys one at a time from Ms. Corry's train to his, saying a number for each key moved], *16, 17, 15, 17, 18, it will be 18 cars long!*

Ms. C: *Now it is really long. Let's count this train together* [Ms. C points to the keys and they count together], *1, 2, 3, 4, 5, 6, 7, 8, 9, 10, 11, 12, 13, 14, 15, 16, 17.*

Here Ms. Corry supported Michael to begin to engage with the idea of combining sets—the specific wording of her question was a productive way to support Michael with a strategy for combining the two sets. Because she asked how long the train would be if her cars "move to your train," Michael followed the story by moving the cars. Ms. Corry did not immediately focus on making sure Michael had the counting sequence correct; instead she wanted to see how he might combine the two sets even before he knew the counting sequence. Even though Michael's counting after 10 did not follow the standard sequence, he showed how he would combine the sets—by first counting his keys and then continue the counting sequence as he moved the keys from Ms. Corry's train to his. To support Michael to develop his counting, she chose to count the keys together with him. This situation could also provide the opportunity to pose other questions to engage Michael in problem solving, such as "How much longer is your train than mine?" or "How many cars would you have left if you attached 3 of your cars to my train?"

Games

Games, particularly linear board games (both commercial and teacher-made), can provide opportunities to support children's counting. In the following vignettes, we see how teachers and children work on counting and how children can extend the counting activities inherent in games to pose problems.

The Shake and Build Game

Ms. Arnold introduced the Shake and Build game at a Family Math Night and, because children and their families enjoyed it so much, she decided to put it in her game center. The game involves rolling a large die and building a tower using the same number of cubes as the numeral shown on the die, and then placing the tower on a mat with squares numbered 1–6 (Figure 5.1). Ms. Arnold's original

Figure 5.1 Building towers

intention was to support children to create sets of given amounts, but while observing, she found that children took the game further—they began to pose their own problems. Ms. Arnold watched Joaquin build a 5 cube tower and then stand it next to a tower of 6 to compare the two.

> **Ms. A:** *I see you're standing your towers up. Can you tell me what you're noticing?*
>
> **Joaquin:** *This tower is 6* [pointing to the 6-cube tower] *and this one* [pointing to the 5-cube tower] *is 1 shorter.*
>
> **Ms. A:** *How tall is this one?* [points to the shorter tower]
>
> **Joaquin:** [points and counts from the bottom up, silently] *It's 5.*
>
> **Ms. A:** *So does that mean that 5 is one less than 6?*
>
> **Joaquin:** [thinking for a minute] *Yes!*
>
> **Ms. A:** *What a cool discovery! Hmm, I wonder how tall your two towers would be together?*
>
> **Joaquin:** [picks up the 6-cube tower] *6* [connects the 5-cube tower to the top of the 6-cube tower, then counts the cubes from the second tower] *7, 8, 9, 10, 11. Now it's 11!*

Ms. Arnold started this exchange by asking Joaquin to explain what he was doing. This question opened the door for her to see how Joaquin was starting to compare the sets by standing the towers next to each other.

The Objects in a Pail Game

Over the course of the year, Ms. Ivy introduces various math games to children. After playing with them, she makes the games available during choice time. Ms. Ivy knows that children often make up their own rules when playing games in her class. Sometimes the new rules provide examples of early problem solving, as was the case when three children in Ms. Ivy's classroom played How Many in a Pail? The game involves using 5 cups numbered 1–5 and a box of craft sticks. Three children went to the table and started their own version of the game by picking a pail, hiding the numeral from the other players, and putting the corresponding number of sticks in the numbered cup. They then took turns asking the other children to guess the numeral based on the sticks. After a few rounds, they decided that they wanted to use all the sticks and put the same number of sticks in each cup. Julia grabbed all of the sticks and distributed them one at a time into each of the 5 cups. After watching for several minutes, Ms. Ivy joined in.

> **Ms. I:** *How many cups do you have?*
>
> **Children:** [each counting the cups] *5.*
>
> **Ms. I:** *How many sticks are in each cup?*
>
> **Children:** [all three children grab a cup and count the sticks—note that only 3 cups of sticks are counted—as each finish counting] *4.*
>
> **Ms. I:** *How many sticks are there altogether?*
>
> **Children:** [dump out all of the sticks and Amy scoops them close to her and begins to count] *There are 20!*

In making this game their own, the children in Ms. Ivy's class were doing much more sophisticated mathematics (even though they might not have been aware of it). Rather than just placing the number of sticks to match the numeral on the cup, the children first figured out a strategy to distribute the sticks into equal amounts in each cup. Ms. Ivy picked up on this and carefully posed questions to get the children to use their counting skills to find out how many sticks were in 5 sets of 4. If she chose to, Ms. Ivy could extend this interaction by restating the problem or having the children do so.

Pretend Contexts

Children frequently engage in counting and problem solving when they are engaged in play with materials that we don't think of as inherently mathematical or when they are making up stories. In this section, we describe several ways we have seen children begin to use their understanding of counting to develop problem-solving skills. As with the earlier examples, a more knowledgeable other—be it teacher, caregiver, another child—often supports the developing understanding through counting with the child to help them learn the sequence or asking questions about what the child is thinking/doing. Although we think it is important to make sure children have access to materials that we often think of as mathematical (e.g., blocks, Legos, games), there are also many opportunities to discuss children's thinking about counting and problem solving when playing with other materials, including items in the kitchen or the doll areas. This is important as some children may be more likely to be socialized to play with the materials we think of as mathematical than others, so we want to purposefully think about the counting and problem solving that are evident in other play areas.

Dramatic Play

The dramatic play area can provide a wealth of counting and problem-solving activities. This makes sense as dramatic play is often a reflection of everyday activities children experience, many of which involve some kind of counting or problem solving. For example, a common activity in dramatic play is "playing store," in which children pretend to make purchases, put prices on items, and exchange money. During this type of play, children may have to consider how much money they have, how much something costs, how much change they should get, and how much they have left after they make a purchase. Another activity we have seen in dramatic play is "nail salon," in which children draw on their experiences observing the everyday practices in a nail salon (because they have family members who either work in a nail salon or get their nails done at a nail salon). In Ms. Schultz's class, children have been using crayons to create various patterns on each other's nails (i.e., one nail is red, one blue, one red, one blue, and so on). Over the period of several days as children play nail salon, their play at "painting" nails sets up the opportunity for Ms. Schultz to ask questions such as: "How many blue nails have you painted?"; "You have painted 4 nails so far. How many more nails do you need to paint if you are going to paint all 10 fingers?"; "You have 4 blue nails, how many are red?"; "Are there more blue or red?"

Using Tools During Dramatic Play

Children often use mathematical tools for their own purposes in pretend play. In Ms. DeBarbieri's classroom, she has ten-frame mats that she tapes onto cookie sheets (Figure 5.2). Sometimes the children in her room use these as ten-frames and sometimes they use them as cookie sheets. One day James and Kazadi filled a cookie sheet ten-frame with magnets and told Ms. DeBarbieri

Figure 5.2 Ten-frame counting

that each magnet was a cookie. They described the kinds of cookies and then delivered them to the children in the book area. When they came back, Kazadi told Ms. DeBarbieri that he has fewer cookies because he gave some away. Ms. DeBarbieri asked Kazadi a series of questions about the number of cookies he started with, how many he gave away, and how many he had left.

These "how many" questions supported Kazadi to reflect on the quantities involved in the situation that emerged through his dramatic play. Because it was set in a context that he devised, the situation made sense to him and he was able to apply his counting skills to solve the questions asked by his teacher. Ms. DeBarbieri could have had a more in-depth conversation about the problem that Kazadi created, but this was his story to narrate—as with all teachers, Ms. DeBarbieri had to make in-the-moment choices about how much to push with math questions and how much to let the play evolve. The cookie sheet ten-frame and magnets are tools that were available for children to take up or not. Although the children in this example used the ten-frame as a cookie sheet, it is often used in this class to hold other items and play other games. The sheet and magnets provided a context that the children were familiar with and seeded ways to support their emerging understanding of ways to make 10.

Blocks and Cars

The block area is a natural place to pose any number of counting questions about the number of blocks being used, how many more blocks one child has compared to a friend, or how many more blocks are needed to make a particular structure. In the following example, we see how Ms. Cooper guided Winnie through a couple of possible scenarios that encouraged Winnie to count and solve problems.

> Winnie had set up an elaborate racetrack in the block area. Ms. Cooper joined in the race car game that required making a car jump over ramps made from cylinder blocks. Winnie was counting the jumps as she went over them, "1, 2, 3, 4, 5, 6, 7, 8." Winnie's friend asked to borrow 2 ramps for a different race track and Ms. Cooper asked Winnie how many she would have left if she gave away 2. Winnie handed 2 to her friend and counted the remaining cylinders and shouted "6, I have 6 tall jumps."

In this example, Winnie took Ms. Cooper's question literally when she asked how many would be left if Winnie gave away 2 ramps. Because there was another friend present to hand the blocks to, this problem became real for Winnie and she could count to solve it. When Ms. Cooper engages with children during their play, she tries to keep the questions close to the child's narrative and plausible within the scene they create. In that way, she provides a realistic opportunity for them to count and solve problems.

These examples show how teachers chose to engage children's mathematical thinking in ways that allowed children to have options about collections they count or ways they play games. These teachers were ready to jump into the play and walked a fine line between taking over and sitting back so that they asked just enough questions. They also made purposeful decisions about what aspects of children's counting and number to focus on. It is important to ask children "How many?" when they are playing with countable materials, but these teachers demonstrated other mathematically productive questions that helped them learn about children's thinking and helped children think about the everyday mathematics they were engaging in. Ms. Schultz asked questions about painting nails that encouraged children to count but also to think about solving a joining problem. Ms. DeBarbieri helped the children to solve a separating problem that reflected what they were doing in their play with cookies. Ms. Corry narrated a story that emerged out of Michael's work counting keys that set him up to think about combining two sets. Ms. Arnold and Ms. Ivy also followed the children's play with games and posed questions that encouraged them to explain the problem solving they were engaging in. These teachers made the activities productive spaces for supporting counting and problem solving. In each case the teacher followed the child's lead and waited until the child did some mathematics, observed what they did, and asked a question related to what the child produced. They started with something the child said or created and identified one aspect of the child's thinking to ask about. There are many other directions the teachers could have taken to support and learn about children's thinking. In the questions for further reflection at the end of the chapter, we offer some other possible responses.

Math Time Activities

There are many small-group and whole-class activities that can be adapted to incorporate counting. We see many teachers and children bring counting into story time. We also see teachers plan for whole-group counting and problem-solving activities.

Counting Collections

Counting collections provides children with opportunities to engage in a variety of practices that support oral counting, grouping, recording, and representing their thinking. Providing a variety of collections to count (e.g., keys, coins, shells, buttons, sticks) and allowing children to choose what and how to count fosters their enthusiasm and agency. Teachers may engage children in counting objects individually or with a partner. Some teachers prefer to work with a small group of children as they count their collections of objects. Other teachers ask the whole class to count collections and often close the activity by having children share how they have counted with their classmates. Teachers often vary the size of the quantities within collections to respond to what they learn about a child's counting. Other teachers provide additional materials to encourage children to count particular features of a collection. Ms. DeBarbieri includes colored paper plates so that children can use the plates to hold their collection (Figure 5.3). What is important is that the children

Figure 5.3 Counting dinosaurs

themselves engage in counting, rather than watching the teacher demonstrate how to count. Although teachers may at times count together with a child, learning about children's thinking requires that teachers observe and respond to each child's varied methods for and ideas about how to count.

The children in Ms. Khan's room work with partners to count collections during small-group time. On this day Nora and Milo are working to count a collection of plastic bears of various colors and sizes.

> **Nora:** [pulling the green bears out of the bag and putting them in a line one at a time] *1, 2, 3, 4, 5, 6.*
>
> **Milo:** [pulling out all of the yellow bears into a pile, and standing each one up as he counts] *1, 2, 3, 4, 5, 6, 7, 8.*
>
> **Ms. K:** *Wow, that is a lot of bears. How many green bears are there?*
>
> [Nora points to each bear while counting silently, while Milo says the numbers out loud.]
>
> **Nora:** *There are 6 green bears.*
>
> **Ms. K:** *How did you know that?*
>
> **Nora:** *Because we counted them!*
>
> **Ms. K:** *Okay, how many yellow bears are there?*
>
> [Nora points while both children say the numbers together.]
>
> **Nora and Milo:** *1, 2, 3, 4, 5, 6, 7, 8—8 bears are yellow.*
>
> **Ms. K:** [gets up to go work with other children] *I wonder how many orange and blue bears there are?*
>
> [The children start lining the other bears up to count.]

The children in Ms. Khan's classroom enjoy selecting things to count. In this situation, Nora and Milo chose to count bears and each picked a color. Ms. Khan posed the questions to both children so she could see different ways the children counted.

There are other questions that she could have posed if she were interested in getting at a different understanding. For example, she might have asked if there were more green bears or more yellow bears. Or she might have asked how many more yellow bears, or how many bears there were altogether (as seen in Chapter 4). As is usually the case, there are numerous questions that you can pose to get at children's thinking. There are no right or wrong questions to ask—it depends on what you know and what you want to know about how the children approach the task.

Conclusion

In this chapter, we have provided a number of examples of how teachers have supported children's mathematical thinking in a variety of instructional spaces by engaging children in creating and posing problems. Although the examples shared here occurred in preschool classrooms, any of them might occur (or could be set up) in older grades, in homes, or in community sites. Although we might not always give children the choice (there are times when we might have specific goals for children's learning), the ideas listed here support children's agency in their learning and identity as young mathematicians.

Questions for Further Reflection

1. Reflect on the spaces we talked about here. What are other spaces in your classroom where you see children engage in mathematics?

2. Take one of the episodes described in this chapter and think of some additional or alternative questions you might ask. How do you think different children in your class might respond to these questions?

3. A commonly used practice during attendance taking is to have children count the number of girls and the number of boys. How might this be problematic? What are other ways to count two different sets of children?

4. Create a new activity similar to the ones described in this chapter that would be appropriate for your class. Try the activity with your class or with some children in your class. How did the children solve the problems you posed?

5. Watch video clip 5.2. How did the teacher negotiate access to the play? When did she back off her questions about counting? Why? What other questions might she have asked?

CLIP 5.2 Water table fill and spill
http://hein.pub/YCM5.2

6. In Chapter 7 we provide more information about the questions teachers ask and why. Reflecting on some of the episodes in this chapter, what different or additional information about children's thinking might you gain from the questions below? What other questions could you ask?

a. In thinking about taking attendance, what kinds of questions might you ask when children are absent?

b. There are many ways Ms. Arnold could have talked to Joaquin about building the towers. She could have continued her line of questioning around "more and less" by asking Joaquin questions such as "If 5 is one less than 6, is 6 one more than 5?" or "What is one less than 5?" She could have asked him questions about the strategy he chose to count all the cubes in the big tower.

c. When Ms. Ivy asked the children about the sticks in a cup, she also could have asked questions to help children reflect on the quantities and actions within the earlier sharing situation such as "How many sticks are there?," "How many cups?," and "How many sticks did you end up putting in each cup?" and then asking something like, "So if you share 20 sticks between 5 cups, how many sticks will you have in each cup?"

References and Further Reading

For more about counting collections:

Schwerdtfeger, J. K., and A. Chan. 2007. "Counting Collections." *Teaching Children Mathematics* 13 (7): 356–61.

For more about board games:

Siegler, R. S., and G. B. Ramani. 2008. "Playing Linear Numerical Board Games Promotes Low-Income Children's Numerical Development." *Developmental Science* 11 (5): 655–61.

Siegler, R. S., and G. B. Ramani. 2009. "Playing Linear Number Board Games—But Not Circular Ones—Improves Low-Income Preschoolers' Numerical Understanding." *Journal of Educational Psychology* 101 (3): 545.

For more about pretend play:

Parks, A. N. 2014. *Exploring Mathematics Through Play in the Early Childhood Classroom.* New York: Teachers College Press.

Parks, A. N., and D. C. Blom. 2014. "Helping Young Children See Math in Play." *Teaching Children Mathematics* 20 (5): 310–17.

6

Solving Story Problems

In Chapters 4 and 5, we discussed how children can use their emerging counting skills to solve problems as they are learning to count. The problems in those two chapters were embedded in counting activities. Children extended their initial counts by adding objects to the collections they had counted, taking objects away, comparing two collections, or grouping objects into equal groups. In this chapter, we discuss how children use essentially the same strategies to solve story problems.

There are important differences between the problems discussed in this chapter and the problems discussed in the two earlier chapters. In the situations that were described in Chapters 4 and 5, children solved problems by organizing and counting the actual things the problems were about (buttons, baseball cards, clothespins, toy animals, toy cars). *With problems discussed in this chapter, children have to construct models of the problem using counters or some other materials that are not the actual things the story is about.* For example, in the first problem in Chapter 4, Yaya had made a collection of 7 buttons, and she had counted them so that she knew there were 7 buttons in the collection. At that point, Mr. McMillan asked, "If you put 2 more buttons with the 7 you have there, how many would you have then?" Yaya was able to solve the problem by adding 2 more buttons to her collection and counting all the buttons. A related story problem might be posed as follows: "Yaya had 7 buttons in her collection. Her teacher gave her 2 more buttons. How many buttons did Yaya have in her collection then?" In this case, the student solving the problem may just have a pile of counters. They do not have buttons. And they are not asked a question about a collection of buttons sitting in front of them. They have to first construct a set of 7 counters to represent the initial collection of 7 buttons, then add 2 counters to the initial set of 7 counters, and then count the resulting set of 9 counters.

Furthermore, they had to plan and execute this entire sequence from a single statement of the problem. For the problems discussed in Chapters 4 and 5, children already had counted or constructed a collection of a given number of objects. Then they were asked to add objects to or remove objects from the collection. As a consequence, they did not have to attend to all elements of a problem at the same time. *For the problems discussed in this chapter, children construct a complete representation from a single statement of the problem* rather than deal with different elements of the problem on a piecemeal basis.

Much of what we cover in this chapter directly parallels the discussion in the preceding chapters, so it will be familiar to you. The problems in Chapters 4 and 5 provide children an easier access to problem solving that lays the groundwork for solving the more abstract problems that are the focus of this chapter. But the distinctions among major problem types and the related strategies for solving them are the same. As you read this chapter, we suggest that you review Chapter 4 to see how the classification of problems and the descriptions of children's strategies for solving them in this chapter correspond to the descriptions of problems and strategies in that chapter.

As we saw in Chapters 4 and 5, the action and relationships described in situations have a direct effect on the strategies young children use to solve problems. Therefore, to understand how children think about and solve different problems, we first need to consider the differences among different types of problems. In the following sections, we describe fundamental distinctions that define different problem types. Most common problem situations that can be solved with arithmetic involve these problem types or combinations of them. In the following discussion we systematically consider the range of problems that children can solve in order to provide a coherent framework for you to use in selecting problems. Although we do not cover all the possible types of problem situations, we include the ones that are the most important for preschool and kindergarten children. For a more complete discussion of problem types, see *Children's Mathematics*.

Addition and Subtraction Problems

We discuss six basic problem types that represent different situations involving addition or subtraction. As adults we consolidate these problem types into the formal operations of addition and subtraction, but children do not initially make sense of problems in these terms. Children's earliest strategies for solving a given problem depend on the action or relationships in the problem situation. As a consequence, understanding the distinctions among problem situations is critical for understanding how children are thinking about and solving a given problem. Addition and subtraction story problems involve four basic kinds of action and relationship: joining and separating actions, and part-part-whole and comparison relationships. Within each of these situations, distinct problem types can be constructed by varying the unknown.

Join and Separate Problems

Consider the three problems in Figure 6.1.

Problem Type	Example
A. Join (Result Unknown)	Carla had 4 trolls. Jude gave her 3 more trolls. How many trolls did Carla have then?
B. Join (Change Unknown)	Carla had 4 trolls. How many more trolls does Carla have to get to have 7 trolls?
C. Separate (Result Unknown)	Carla had 7 trolls. She gave 4 of her trolls to Jude. How many trolls did Carla have then?

Figure 6.1 Join and Separate problems

If you were asked which two of the problems in Figure 6.1 are most alike, you might respond in several ways. You might say that B and C are most alike, because they both could be solved (by adults) by subtracting. You might say that A and B are most alike, because in each case Carla is given more trolls. Or you might say that A and C are the most alike, because the answer is the number of trolls that Carla ends up with. A case can be made for all three choices.

Problems A and B are both Join problems. In both problems, Carla initially had 4 trolls and was given 3 more. The difference between A and B is what is known and what is unknown. In A, the number of trolls that Carla had to start with and the number she is given are listed in the problem statement. The number of trolls Carla wound up with is the unknown. In B, the number of trolls that Carla had to start with and the number she wanted to have are given in the problem statement. The number of trolls that Carla needed to add to her collection to have 7 trolls altogether is the unknown. In both problems, there is action that involves joining something to the initial quantity. In problem C, the action involves taking something away from the initial quantity rather than adding something to it. As with problem A, the answer to problem C is the result at the end after the action has taken place. The result of the action is the unknown. Thus we call this a Separate (Result Unknown) problem.

Additional Join and Separate problems can be constructed by varying the unknown, but the three problems in Figure 6.1 are the most important for young children.

Part-Part-Whole Problems

Examples of the two Part-Part-Whole problem types are given in Figure 6.2. Part-Part-Whole problems are different from the Join and Separate problems in that no action is described. Nothing is being eaten or collected; rather, we have 3 roses and 4 tulips and want to know how many flowers. These problems describe the numerical relations between a quantity and the two parts that make up the whole quantity. In the Part-Part-Whole (Whole Unknown) problem, the two parts are given (roses and tulips) and the whole is the unknown (flowers). In the Part-Part-Whole (Part Unknown) problem, the whole (flowers) and one of the parts (roses) are given, and the goal is to find the other part (tulips). To keep things simple, we did not discuss

Unknown	Example
Whole	Elise has 4 tulips and 3 roses. How many flowers does Elise have altogether?
Part	Elise has 7 flowers. 4 are tulips and the rest are roses. How many roses does Elise have?

Figure 6.2 Part-Part-Whole problems

Part-Part-Whole problems in Chapter 4, but Part-Part-Whole situations do arise in counting activities. For example, if a child is counting colored bears and has made a set of 7 blue bears and 4 red bears, you might ask how many blue bears there are, how many red bears, and how many bears altogether.

These problems may seem a lot like the Join and Separate problems, but there are important differences. Part-Part-Whole problems do not describe any action relating the parts and the whole. Furthermore, the actions in Join and Separate problems take place over time. There is an initial quantity at Time 1. Something is added to it or removed from it during Time 2, and the result is a new quantity at Time 3. There is no such temporal element in Part-Part-Whole problems. A third difference between the problems is that with Join (Result Unknown) problems, the initial quantity and the quantity that is joined to it (the change) play quite different roles. A young child might not recognize that joining 2 to 7 and joining 7 to 2 will result in the same answer. In Part-Part-Whole problems, the two parts play essentially the same role.

Compare Problems

Compare problems also do not involve any action, but the relation is between two sets rather than between a set and its parts. The basic question for Compare problems is how much more there is in one set than another.

> *Jennifer has 7 trolls. Sofia has 4 trolls. How many more trolls does Jennifer have than Sofia?*

As was the case with Join and Separate problems, additional types of Compare problems can be constructed by varying the unknown, but the above Compare problem is the most accessible for young children and is the most common comparison problem situation encountered outside of school.

Summary of Addition and Subtraction Problem Types

Examples of each of the problems are given in Figure 6.3. Attending to these problem structures allows us see how children naturally draw upon their understandings of these actions and relationships to solve problems and develop a foundation for learning formal arithmetic. Although there are some additional types of addition and subtraction problems, these six types are the most important for children at the preschool and kindergarten levels.

Action/Relation		
Join	*Join (Result Unknown)* Gabriela had 3 action figures. Sheryl just gave her 2 more action figures. How many action figures does Gabriela have now?	*Join (Change Unknown)* Gabriela has 3 action figures. How many more action figures does Gabriela have to get to have 5 altogether?
Separate	*Separate (Result Unknown)* Gabriela had 5 action figures. She gave 2 action figures to Sheryl. How many action figures does Gabriela have now?	
Part-Part-Whole	*Part-Part-Whole (Whole Unknown)* Gabriela has 3 blue action figures and 2 red action figures. How many action figures does Gabriela have altogether?	*Part-Part-Whole (Part Unknown)* Gabriela has 5 action figures. 3 are blue and the rest are red. How many red action figures does Gabriela have?
Compare	Gabriela has 5 action figures. Sheryl has 3 action figures. How many more action figures does Gabriela have than Sheryl?	

Figure 6.3 Six basic addition and subtraction problem types

CLIP 6.1 Daniel solves joining and separting problems
http://hein.pub/YCM6.1

CLIP 6.2 Mohammad solves a separating problem
http://hein.pub/YCM6.2

Children's Addition and Subtraction Strategies

Direct Modeling Strategies

Children are good at attending to the action or relation in a problem and doing what the problem says to do. They consistently use strategies that reflect the action or relations described in the problems. Children initially use fingers, counters, or paper and marker to directly represent the quantities, the action on the quantities, and the relations among quantities described in the problems. We call these strategies Direct Modeling strategies. Examples of these strategies follow.

Children solve the Join (Result Unknown) and Part-Part-Whole (Whole Unknown) problems using similar strategies. They use counters or fingers to represent each of the sets and then count the total number of objects in the two sets combined. For example, consider the following problem:

> *Peggy had 6 stickers. She bought 3 more stickers. How many stickers did she have then?*

Dion made a set of 6 cubes and another set of 3 cubes. He pushed the two sets together and counted all the cubes in the combined set, "1, 2, 3, 4, 5, 6, 7, 8, 9" pointing at each cube as he counted it. He then answered, "She had 9."

Bridget used a very similar strategy to solve the following Join (Change Unknown) problem.

> *Peggy has 6 stickers. How many more stickers does she need to buy to have 9 stickers?*

Bridget first made a set of 6 cubes. She then added cubes until there were a total of 9. As she added the additional cubes, she counted "7, 8, 9." As she was adding the cubes to make a total of 9, she kept the added cubes separate from the initial set of

6 cubes so that she could count the cubes she added on. She then looked at the 3 cubes she had added and answered, "She needs 3 more."

There is quite a bit more involved in solving the Join (Change Unknown) problem than is involved in solving the Join (Result Unknown) problem. To solve the Join (Change Unknown) problem, Bridget had to plan ahead. She had to keep the cubes that she added on separate from the 6 cubes in the original set. Some children accurately model the problem but fail to keep the cubes they add on separate from the original set so that they cannot figure out how many cubes they added.

Children solve Separate (Result Unknown) problems by making a set representing the initial quantity given in the problem; taking away the number of cubes that represents the number given away, lost, eaten, and so on, and counting the remaining cubes. For example, consider Arun's solution to the following problem:

> **Peggy had 8 stickers. She gave 6 stickers to a friend. How many stickers did she have then?**

Arun made a collection of 8 cubes. He removed 6 of them and counted the remaining cubes, responding, "She was nice to her friend. She just had 2 stickers left, and her friend got 6."

Because there is no explicit action in the problem, Part-Part-Whole (Part Unknown) problems tend to be more difficult than the Join and Separate problems. Students who do solve Part-Part-Whole (Part Unknown) problems generally use the same strategy they would use for the Separate problem or the strategy they would use for the Join (Change Unknown) problem.

By kindergarten, many children can solve Compare problems by matching two sets representing the two numbers given in the problem, as in the following example.

> **Peggy has 8 stickers. Sonja has 6 stickers. Who has more stickers? How many more stickers does Peggy have than Sonja?**

Tiana made a set of 8 cubes and a set of 6 cubes. She lined them up so that 6 of the cubes in the set of 8 were aligned with the set of 6 cubes (see Figure 6.4). She then counted the cubes that were not matched and responded, "2 more."

Figure 6.4 A matching strategy for comparing 8 and 6

Counting On Strategies

We have described the Direct Modeling strategies that young children use to solve various problems. These strategies are productive for children and they support them to adapt their strategies to more sophisticated ones. Children typically transition from a Direct Modeling strategy to a Counting On strategy. When children use a Counting On strategy, they are continuing to follow the action in the problem (as they did with their Direct Modeling strategy) but they now recognize that they do not have to recount the counters that they have already counted.

Over time, children adapt these strategies to make them even more efficient. For example, consider the progression of children's strategies for the following Join (Result Unknown) problem.

> *Peggy had 6 stickers. She bought 2 more stickers. How many stickers did she have then?*

In directly modeling this problem, children make a set of 6 counters and another set of 2 counters. They then count all the counters in the two sets starting at 1 — "1, 2, 3, 4, 5, 6, 7, 8" — even though they have already counted the 6 counters in the first set. At some point, children recognize that they do not have to recount the initial set. They can point to the first set and say "6" and count on from there "7, 8." Soon they come to recognize that they do not even need to construct the initial set; they can just count on from 6. For example, in solving this problem, Kate did not make either set. She started with the number 6 and counted on. She said, "6 [pause], 7, 8. The answer is 8." As she said "7, 8" she raised a finger with each count to keep track of the number of counting words she had said. When she had 2 fingers raised, she knew that she had counted on 2 beyond 6 and that the number she had reached was the total.

Children use a similar Counting strategy for Join (Change Unknown) problems. For the following Join (Change Unknown) problem, children would also count on from 6 to 8, but the goal is to count from 6 to 8, not to count on 2 more from 6. The number of counts beyond 6 is the unknown. The answer is the number of counting words after 6 rather than the last number counted.

> **Peggy has 6 stickers. How many more stickers does she need to buy to have 8 stickers?**

Note both these strategies still reflect the structure of the problem. Counting on is an abstraction of the Direct Modeling strategies used to solve Join problems. Counting on is easiest if the number to count on is 1 or 2, and possibly 3. For small numbers like these, keeping track of the number counted on is relatively easy. For example, a number of young children might recognize that the solution to the following problem is 8, because 8 is the next counting number after 7.

> **Jaiden had 7 flowers. She picked 1 more flower. How many flowers did she have then?**

Children also use a Counting Back strategy for Separate (Result Unknown) problems that reflects the structure of those problems. But counting back is quite a bit harder than counting on, and not all children count back to solve Separate (Result Unknown) problems. Relatively few preschool or kindergarten children do so. (For a more in depth discussion of counting strategies, see *Children's Mathematics*).

Number Facts

Some preschool and kindergarten children know some number facts and can use them to solve problems. Facts involving doubles ($2 + 2, 4 + 4, 7 + 7$, and so on) and adding 1 ($5 + 1, 7 + 1$, and so on) are commonly learned before most other facts. Some young children are able to use the facts they know to derive number facts that they do not know. For example, a child may figure out $4 + 5$ by recognizing that it is 1 more than $4 + 4$. Children may also know sums to 10 and use this knowledge to derive other facts. For example, a child may figure out the answer to $8 + 5$ by drawing on knowledge that $8 + 2 = 10$, taking 2 from the 5 to add to the 8 to get 10, and then adding 10 to the 3 that is left to get 13. Derived number facts play an important role in the learning of number facts by older children.

Relative Difficulty of Problems

Recognizing that young children solve problems by modeling the action and relations in the problems provides a gauge for assessing the relative difficulty of different problems. The relevant factors are *how apparent the action or relationship described in a given problem is* and *how difficult is it to represent the action or relationship*.

The Join (Result Unknown) and the Separate (Result Unknown) problems have relatively obvious action that is easy to model, and as might be expected they are two of the easiest addition and subtraction problem types. The Part-Part-Whole (Whole Unknown) type is solved in essentially the same way as the Join (Result Unknown) problem, and there is not a great deal of difference in difficulty between the two. Part-Part-Whole (Part Unknown) problems can be quite a bit more difficult than any of the other problems we have discussed because there is no action to support the child to know what to do with the quantities. We have included a discussion of Part-Part-Whole (Part Unknown) problems because it is easy to confuse them with Join (Change Unknown) or Separate (Result Unknown) problems, and young children often struggle with them.

Compare problems also include no action, and the Matching strategy that directly represents the comparison relationship is less obvious and harder for young children to apply than the strategies they use to solve Join and Separate problems. As a consequence, these problems also tend to be more difficult than the Join and Separate problems described here. Nevertheless, children as young as kindergarten age can solve Compare problems by Matching if they have appropriate opportunities to solve a variety of problems, and even preschool children can begin to engage successfully with comparison situations as described in the discussion of comparison strategies above. In fact, most of the problems discussed in this chapter can be approached at some level by many preschool children and most kindergarten children.

Multiplication and Division

Many curriculum guidelines and textbooks presume that instruction in arithmetic should start with addition and subtraction (or just addition) and that multiplication and division should be deferred to the second or third grade. In part, this decision has been based on the assumption that multiplication and division are too difficult for young children to understand. This turns out to be an invalid assumption. Young children can, in fact, solve a variety of multiplication and division story problems using modeling processes similar to those they use for addition and subtraction. In fact, multiplication and division problems may be easier for young children than some addition and subtraction problems. We argue that young children should be introduced to multiplication and division situations from the beginning. They often

CLIP 6.3 Hazel solves a multiplication problem
http://hein.pub/YCM6.3

CLIP 6.4 Mohammad solves a multiplication problem
http://hein.pub/YCM6.4

encounter these problems in their everyday experiences and in counting collections. We are not proposing that young children need to learn formal symbols (×, ÷) for multiplication and division, but we believe they should have experience with problems that involve grouping and partitioning.

We are not recommending that we introduce children to multiplication and division problems just because they *can* solve them. Including multiplication and division problems provides children a richer and more complete problem-solving experience that supports thoughtful analysis of problem situations. It provides opportunity for children to extend and articulate their intuitive modeling practices. As a consequence, including multiplication and division may actually help children to develop deeper understanding of addition and subtraction. Another compelling reason to include grouping problems is that grouping underlies concepts of place value, and it makes a lot of sense to give children general experience with grouping before they have to deal with the specific demands of grouping by tens. We are not proposing that place value should be formally taught in preschool, but we believe we should be laying the groundwork for it.

Grouping and Partitioning Problems

Consider the following problem situation:

> *Trentin had 12 candies. He put the candies in 3 boxes.*
> *He put 4 candies in each box.*

There are three quantities in the problem: the total number of candies, the number of boxes, and the number of candies in each box. From this basic situation, we can create three different problems by varying which two quantities are known and which is the unknown (Figure 6.5). We have named the problem types to facilitate the discussion of them, but we are not suggesting that you use these names with children.

For the Multiplication problem, the number of groups and the number of objects in each group are given. The unknown is the total number of objects (how many total candies). The two given numbers in a multiplication problem represent two distinct quantities: the number of groups and the number of objects in each group. This distinction is important, because children treat the two quantities differently.

For the Measurement Division problem, the total number of objects and the number of objects in each group are given, and the unknown is the number of groups (how many boxes filled). You can think of children measuring out the number of objects in each group to find the unknown number of groups. That is where the name Measurement Division comes from.

For the Partitive Division problem, the total number of objects and the number of groups are given, and the unknown is the number of objects in each group (how many candies are in each box). The objects are essentially partitioned into equal-sized groups, hence the name Partitive Division.

Problem Type	Example
Multiplication	Trentin had 3 boxes of candy. He put 4 candies into each box. How many candies did he put into the boxes?
Measurement Division	Trentin had 12 candies. He put 4 candies into each box. How many boxes did he fill?
Partitive Division	Trentin had 12 candies. He put the candies into 3 boxes with the same number of candies in each box. How many candies did he put into each box?

Figure 6.5 Multiplication and division problem types

Direct Modeling Strategies

As with addition and subtraction problems, young children solve multiplication and division problems by directly modeling the action in the problem. Eventually they start to use skip counting strategies and number facts, but these more abstract strategies are not used by many preschool or kindergarten children. As a consequence, we limit our discussion of multiplication and division strategies to Direct Modeling.

Multiplication

Children directly model the groupings in the Multiplication problem by making the given number of groups with the same number in each group. The following is an example of how Emily solved a Multiplication problem.

> **There are 3 tennis balls in a can. How many balls are there in 6 cans?**

Emily makes 6 piles of cubes with 3 cubes in each pile. She counts the total number of cubes and responds, "18." Note Emily very clearly makes 6 piles with 3 cubes in each pile. It would be very unusual for a child to make 3 piles with 6 cubes in each pile for this problem. In fact, if given the following problem, most young children would not recognize that it had the same answer as the tennis ball problem.

> **There are 6 pieces of gum in each package. How many pieces of gum are in 3 packages?**

Measurement Division

Children solve Measurement Division problems by making sets of the given size and counting the sets they have made. There are several variants to this solution that are illustrated below.

> **Rebecca plans to take cupcakes to the school bake sale. She has 15 cupcakes. She wants to put 3 cupcakes on each plate. How many plates does Rebecca need for her cupcakes?**

Zara counts out 15 cubes. Then she puts them in piles of 3 until they are all used up. She counts the number of piles and responds, "5."

   Carmen counts the counters as she is making the piles. Because the number in each pile is small, it is easy for her to see when she has put enough in a pile. She makes the first pile, counting, "1, 2, 3." She makes the next pile, counting, "4, 5, 6."

She continues this way, counting, "7, 8, 9" for the third pile, "10, 11, 12" for the fourth pile, and "13, 14, 15" for the last pile. When she gets to 15 she knows to stop making piles and counts the number of piles she has made. She responds, "5 plates."

Note that Zara first counts out a collection of cubes to represent the total number of cupcakes and then puts them into piles of the given size, while Carmen keeps track of the number of cubes she is putting out as she is making the piles.

Partitive Division

Children solve Partitive Division problems by distributing the given total into a given number of groups and counting the objects in each group. There are also variations of the modeling strategy for this problem, but they essentially represent the same kind of grouping.

> *Aki took brownies to the bake sale. She baked 12 brownies. She put the brownies on 3 plates so that there was the same number of brownies on each plate. How many brownies did she put on each plate?*

Neevah counts out 12 blocks. She has a pile of plates from which she selects 3. She puts 1 cube on the first plate, 1 on the second, and 1 on the third. Then she starts over, putting 1 more cube on each plate. She continues this way until the cubes are all used up. She then counts the cubes on each plate and responds, "4."

Malik also counts out 12 blocks, but instead of dealing the blocks out one by one, he makes 3 piles with 3 blocks in each pile. When he sees that he has not used up all the blocks, he adds one more block to each pile. He then counts the blocks in each pile and responds, "4."

Children can use a variety of tools to solve multiplication and division problems. If they have paper and a marker, they may draw a circle to represent the groups and then put the given number of objects in each circle either by drawing them or by putting counters in the circles. Providing containers such as small cups can make it easier for the children to get started modeling multiplication and division problems, but after experience with these problems, children usually do not need containers for very long.

Division Problems with Remainders

For all of the division problems we have discussed so far, the division comes out even with nothing left over, but not all problem situations that we encounter are so straightforward. Children can also solve problems that have remainders, like the problems in Figure 6.6. With young children, we recommend starting with story problems that do not have remainders. However, problems that arise naturally in class may have remainders, and it is not unreasonable to have a discussion of what to do with them. The problems in Figure 6.6 require different ways of dealing with remainders. In the first problem, the answer is 3 stickers. 17 divided by 5 is 3 with a remainder of 2. But the 2 extra stickers cannot be equally shared among 5 students, so the remainder of 2 is essentially ignored. In the second problem, the answer is 5 cars. 18 divided by 4 is 4 with a remainder of 2. But in this case, we cannot leave the 2 students behind so another car is needed.

Ms. K has 17 stickers that she wants to share with 5 students in her class. How many stickers can she give to each student so that each student gets the same number of stickers?

18 children are going to the zoo. 4 children can ride in each car. How many cars will be needed to get all the children to the zoo?

Figure 6.6 Division problems with remainders

Teacher Reflection

I started with sharing (Partitive Division) problems that all revolved around sharing snacks or small toys. Let me tell you, there was not one child that could not divide up the objects fairly. They also had no problem telling me how many they each had. It was the perfect place for me to get some entry data on what my students understood. I quickly found that numbers above 10 were where I would see differences in their understanding. But even those who could not always count with one-to-one correspondence could still divide up the objects and count the smaller sets. After a few of these problems, I started mixing up the different problem types and continued that way for the rest of the year.

—**Anna Navarro,** *preschool and kindergarten teacher*

Teacher Reflections

Prior to introducing Cognitively Guided Instruction (CGI) into my classroom, the curriculum I used did not offer students the opportunity to solve "nonkindergarten" problems. The opportunity to go far beyond what was expected was nearly nonexistent, and to even consider presenting multiplication or division word problems to kindergarteners seemed ridiculous and nonsensical. However, the practice and philosophy of CGI has now proven otherwise in my classroom. Why ask kindergarten students to solve "nonkindergarten" problems like multiplication and division? Because they *can* solve these types of word problems!

I truly believe that "opportunity" is a key concept within the entire process and purpose of CGI. You can't know what students can or cannot do unless you provide the opportunity for them to show their ability. Traditional ideas of differentiation and enrichment cannot reach the caliber that CGI offers. CGI and the exposure to joining, separating, multiplying, and dividing offer educators and students the chance to go beyond what is expected. It allows for the possibility of students to surpass grade-level standards and use their natural math skill set to solve problems that they may not typically be expected to solve.

—**Courtney Farrar,** *kindergarten teacher*

Making Story Problems Easier and More Accessible

In Chapter 4 we discussed how children solved problems set in the context of learning to count. Those problems provide a good starting place for children to use their emerging counting abilities to solve problems. Asking children to solve story problems may initially prove challenging because there is a great deal for children to attend to and manage and because you are asking children to solve problems in ways that make sense to them rather than showing them how to solve the problem. If a child is struggling with a particular problem, there are a number of ways that you can scaffold the problem solving process to provide the child with support to engage with the problem.

Understanding the Problem Context

For children to successfully solve a problem, they must understand the problem context. They must understand the nature of the action or relationships described in the problem in order to model it. Real situations in which children solve a problem to get an answer that has meaning for them can both motivate children to solve the problem and provide a context that the children understand. For example, deciding how many treats to bring so that each child gets 3 is a problem that could provide a meaningful context. Story problems that involve familiar situations with familiar actions help children to understand what a problem is describing. For example, problems in which children give something away, lose something, or eat something might be situations where children will recognize that something is being taken away from an initial quantity.

It also can be fruitful to discuss the problem situation in some detail before asking children to solve the problem. Take the problem posed earlier in this chapter: *There are 6 pieces of gum in each package. How many pieces of gum are in 3 packages?* Before inviting children to solve the problem, a teacher might ask children to talk about what the story is about and to describe what is happening in the story. The goal of the discussion would be to make sure that children understand the story context so they can use this understanding to make sense of the mathematical relationship within the problem (in this case, that there are groups and that each group contains the same number of items). Asking children to talk about the story in their own words supports them to focus on the situation (rather than key words) and to share what they understand about the story. Often children's initial response may be that the story is about gum. A teacher might build on this response by asking the child and the class to say more: "What about the gum? What is a package? Can you think of any examples of packages? What kind of gum might it be?" And so on. Note that these questions are not about the numbers in isolation or about how to solve the problem. Focusing on understanding the story will help children elaborate on the context and make sense of it for themselves. It will also help them see that the numbers in the story represent two different things (packs and pieces of gum), and therefore that counting the 3 packs and the 6 pieces together to get 9 does not make sense.

Discrete Objects

Problems that are about discrete objects that can be counted may be easier for young children to model than problems about measures that are not directly observable, like time, distance, length, or weight. For example, the first problem below could be easier to model directly than the second.

> *Jessica had 5 fish. Her friends gave her 3 more fish for her birthday. How many fish did she have then?*
>
> *Tim's new puppy weighed 5 pounds when Tim got her. She has gained 3 pounds. How much does the puppy weigh now?*

Selection of Numbers

The numbers in a problem can affect the difficulty of the problem. As might be expected, problems with smaller numbers tend to be easier than problems with larger numbers. Children often can solve problems involving numbers less than 10 by representing the numbers with their fingers. On the other hand, if the numbers are too small, it can be difficult to figure out how a child might have solved a particular problem, and the child might not get much opportunity to think about how they solved the problem. Children often can solve problems with larger numbers, as long as all the numbers in the problem (including the answer) are within the children's comfortable counting range and they have appropriate tools to solve the problem. Textbooks often start with very small numbers and work up one number at a time. But we recommend trying a range of numbers to see what works for your students.

Providing Appropriate Tools

Children may have an easier time solving a problem if they have tools that make it easier to model the problem. For example, children may have more success solving Grouping and Partitioning problems if they have containers that they can put counters in to represent the groups. Children also can use paper and markers to represent containers. The discussion of children's strategies for the Partitive Division problem earlier in this chapter illustrates how appropriate tools can make a problem more accessible.

Breaking Up the Problem

If a child is having difficulty with a problem, you might break the problem up and ask the child to represent part of it. For example, consider the following exchange. Freddie was unable to get started on the problem, so Mr. Zinn engaged her in the following conversation.

> ### Mio had 7 cookies. She ate 2 of them. How many cookies did Mio have left?

> **Mr. Z:** *Let me read the problem to you again. "Mio had 7 cookies." Pretend that the blocks are cookies. Can you use these blocks to show me Mio's cookies?*

> [Freddie pulls out 7 blocks.]

Mr. Z: *Good. Now, Mio ate 2 of them. Can you show me that?*

[Freddie takes 2 of the blocks away.]

Mr. Z: *Okay. Now how many cookies does Mio have left?*

Freddie: [counts the remaining blocks] *5.*

You need to be careful in breaking problems up for students, and you want to be careful to avoid overusing the practice. When you break up a problem, you are doing some of the most critical work for a student, and you want them to take on that work for themselves as soon as and as much as possible.

Engaging a Child Who Has No Idea How to Begin

Sometimes a child may have no idea how to begin on a problem. A goal for that child is to get them to engage with the problem. Breaking it up and asking the child to model just a part of the problem is one approach for getting children to start to represent a problem, but sometimes that is not enough. Consider the following problem:

> **Finn has 8 action figures. How many more action figures does he need to get so he will have 11 action figures?**

If a child is struggling to solve this problem and cannot decide what to do after making an initial set of 8 blocks, you might ask whether they would have enough if they got 1 more action figure. After the child tries adding 1 block and finds that there are only 9 blocks, you could ask what they might do next, providing support as needed to get them to recognize that they could add another block and then another until there are 11 blocks.

Math Story Time

Mar Jensen was interested in how teachers could engage young children in problem-solving activities in ways that were developmentally responsive. Rather than *reading* a story problem, she suggests having children *act out* the story problem. One of the

(continues)

benefits of this practice is that it provides children an opportunity to engage in the activity at multiple levels. Another teacher we work with, Renae DeBarbieri, has modified the idea and made it a regular practice in her prekindergarten (age four years) classroom. She calls it "Math Story Time."

Planning the problem. Ms. DeBarbieri introduces math story time to her class gradually, over the course of the year, adding in more complex problems as children develop understanding. In terms of context, she usually starts with a theme the children are interested in.

The barnyard story. After reading several books about farms, Ms. DeBarbieri set up a series of problems about a farmer and farm animals. Before students arrived she used painter's tape to mark off two large rectangles on the floor. During circle time, she told the children that they were going to do a story about a barnyard. She explained that the large rectangle was the pasture for the cows and the smaller rectangle was the pen. She told the children she would need 9 actors for that day's show. (Ms. DeBarbieri makes sure that every child gets to perform over the course of the week.) She called up children one at a time, stopping a few times along the way to have the children count the actors already selected. Once there were 9 children on the "stage," Ms. DeBarbieri shared the story.

Ms. D: *Farmer Carp has 9 cows in his cow pen* [points to the cow pen rectangle].

[All the children on the stage scurry into the area marked off for the cow pen.]

Ms. D: *Let's count the cows in the pen* [children are on their hands and knees crawling around mooing]. *How are we going to count these wiggly cows?*

Children: *Make them stand still. Give them hay so they stop walking.*

Ms. D: *Okay cows, let's line up at this fence for your lunch* [children crawl over and get in line]. *Help me count these cows.*

Anya: [one of the cows in the middle of the line starts counting] *1, 2, 3, 4, I'm 5, 6, 7, 8, 9* [other children in the class are also counting].

Ms. D: *Okay, do we agree, we have 9 cows?*

Children: *Yes!*

Ms D: *Back to our story. Farmer Carp opens the gate to go in the pen but she trips over a bucket* [pretends to trip], *and before she can get up, 3 cows escape into the pasture.*

[Ms. DeBarbieri has found over time that it is helpful to prepare some of the actors by setting up part of the story ahead of time—in this case, telling three of the children they would be escaping. Ms. DeBarbieri points one at a time to the runaway cows as they crawl out of the pen into the pasture.]

Ms. D: *There goes 1 cow, there goes* [looks to the audience to chime in].

Children: *2 cows, there goes 3 cows.*

Ms. D: [pretending to close a gate] *Now the gate is closed. Let's talk about this story. How many cows did the farmer have to start?*

Children: *9 cows.*

(continues)

Ms. D: *How many cows got out into the pasture?* [walks over and holds her hand over each cow as the class counts to 3] *How are we going to find out how many cows are left in the pen?*

Children: [calling out at once] *Count them! 7! 6!*

Ms. D: *I heard some people say 7, I heard some people say 6, I heard some say we need to count them.*

[At this point Ms. DeBarbieri has children who called out a number share how they got that number, and then the class counts the remaining cows to get 6.]

Ms. D: *So if there were 9 cows in the pen and 3 got out to the pasture, how many cows did we have left in the pen?*

Children: *6!*

Conclusion: Building on Children's Intuitive Strategies

As we have seen in this chapter and in preceding chapters, young children know a lot more about fundamental ideas underlying arithmetic than we typically have given them credit for. We want to support children to build upon and extend their informal strategies both to develop understanding for arithmetic that is consistent with the ways they naturally think and to foster their problem solving. Children do not have to be shown how to use these strategies, and optimally, they are not formally taught. When strategies are shared with the class, children may learn from one another, but we have found it best that the teacher not demonstrate a strategy for the children to adopt and implement. When another child shows their strategy, students get to see one possible way to solve a problem and it provides room for other children to solve and share other strategies. When a teacher demonstrates a strategy, there is a risk that children will assume that strategy is the way the problem should be solved and try to imitate the strategy whether they understand it or not.

With traditional instruction children first learn to add, subtract, multiply, and divide and then apply the skills they have been taught to solve corresponding story problems. We recommend turning the process around, using children's intuitive problem-solving strategies to develop understanding of the operations of addition, subtraction, multiplication, and division before we introduce the formal symbols and algorithms. Several compelling reasons support this approach. First of all, understanding develops when new knowledge is connected to existing knowledge. Children can understand joining, separating, grouping, and partitioning before they are formally introduced to the mathematical notation that is used to represent these operations. It makes a lot of sense to build on this foundation. Furthermore, if the formal operations are not connected to these intuitive notions, there is evidence that children will construct two somewhat isolated systems of arithmetic: one that makes sense to them and that they use to solve problems in the real world and one that they use for school mathematics that follows a seemingly arbitrary set of rules.

Another reason it makes sense to start with the strategies children intuitively use to solve arithmetic problems is that the general modeling strategy that comes naturally to young children represents a good general problem-solving strategy that is based on understanding the problem situation. While the most serious difficulty that older children experience with arithmetic is applying what they know to solve problems, young children are actually good problem solvers. If older children applied some of the strategies they intuitively used when they were younger, they would be much more successful problem solvers. Too often older children whose knowledge of addition, subtraction, multiplication, and division is not connected to their intuitive conceptions of these operations attempt to solve problems by using strategies that focus on superficial features of problems, such as key words or adding when there are three or more numbers in the problem. Although these shorthand approaches or tricks may work in the short run, they often do not work in later problem solving and they keep children from building on their own intuitive understandings.

Solving problems can be regularly embedded in everyday activity, and the analysis of children's solutions provides a basis for understanding how children may react to problems that occur in their everyday experiences. In fact, many of the everyday situations that provide opportunities for counting often involve solving some sort of problem. Children, regardless of their level of understanding, can learn from participating in solving problems. Even if they cannot solve a given problem themselves, children can learn from participating in problem-solving activity, listening to other children discussing their solutions, and even asking questions that help others understand more.

Although quite young children can solve a variety of problems involving addition, subtraction, multiplication, and division, it is not necessary to introduce formal symbols ($+, -, \times, \div$) for these operations in preschool. Some children may have learned them outside of school, and that is fine. But the goal for preschool and kindergarten should be to help children apply their intuitive strategies to a variety of problems and be able to show and describe them. At the preschool and kindergarten levels, we should be building a foundation that will support children to continue to develop understanding and learn skills with understanding. We want children to see themselves as able to make sense of arithmetic, discover new ideas, and use their growing knowledge to solve problems in ways that are consistent with their intuitive problem-solving strategies.

Research Summary

The results of a study that was conducted with kindergarten children (Carpenter et al. 1993) are summarized in Figure 6.7. This study found that, by the end of kindergarten, children in CGI classes could solve a variety of problems by modeling the action or relations described in the problems. Many teachers and curriculum developers considered the problems too difficult for young children, but the results provided compelling support that children as young as kindergarten age can invent strategies to solve a variety of problems if they are given the opportunity to do so. In almost every case, the children used the Direct Modeling strategies predicted by our model of the development of children's mathematical thinking.

Problem	Percentage of Children Who Solved Problem Correctly	Percentage of Children Who Used a Valid Strategy*
Paco had 13 cookies. He ate 6 of them. How many cookies does Paco have left?	73	89
Carla has 7 dollars. How many more dollars does she have to earn so that she will have 11 dollars to buy a puppy?	74	80
James has 12 balloons. Amy has 7 balloons. How many more balloons does James have than Amy?	67	71
Robin has 3 packages of gum. There are 6 pieces of gum in each package. How many pieces of gum does Robin have altogether?	71	86
Tad had 15 guppies. He put 3 guppies in each jar. How many jars did Tad put guppies in?	71	73
Mr. Gomez had 20 cupcakes. He put the cupcakes into 4 boxes so that there were the same number of cupcakes in each box. How many cupcakes did Mr. Gomez put in each box?	70	70
19 children are going to the circus. 5 children can ride in each car. How many cars will be needed to get all 19 children to the circus?	64	64
Maria had 3 packages of cupcakes. There were 4 cupcakes in each package. She ate 5 cupcakes. How many are left?	64	67
19 children are taking a minibus to the zoo. The bus has 7 seats. How many children will have to sit 3 to a seat, and how many can sit 2 to a seat?	51	59

*Includes children who solved correctly as well as those who would have solved correctly except for a minor counting error

Figure 6.7 Kindergarten children's success in solving various story problems

Questions for Further Reflection

1. Identify the problem type for each of the following problems.

   a. Marsha has 9 apples. 2 are red and the rest are green. How many green apples does Marsha have?

   b. Ramos wants to buy a game that costs 8 dollars. He has saved 3 dollars. How many more dollars does Ramos need to save to be able to buy the game?

   c. Felicia has 9 stickers. Susan has 6 stickers. How many more stickers does Felicia have than Susan?

   d. Juan has made 12 muffins out of play dough. He wants to give the muffins to 3 friends so that each person gets the same number of muffins. How many muffins will each child get?

   e. Jazmine is counting buttons. She has taken out 12 red buttons and 8 blue buttons. She gives 5 of her red buttons to Sarah. How many red buttons does Jazmine have left?

2. Describe how children might solve the problems in question 1.

3. Write a problem illustrating each of the problem types described in this chapter.

4. Describe how children in your class might solve the problems you wrote.

5. Give the problems to several children you think might be able to solve them. Describe the strategies they use.

6. If a child struggled to solve a particular problem, how did you provide support so that they might solve the problem?

7. For each of the problems in Chapter 4 that corresponds to a problem type discussed in this chapter, identify the problem type.

8. For each of the problems in Chapter 5 that corresponds to a problem type discussed in this chapter, identify the problem type.

9. Look at the example in Chapter 7 showing how Ms. Farrar interacted with Isaac to help him understand the problem situation (p. 106). What other questions might she have asked to help a student understand the problem?

10. For one of the problems you wrote for question 3, describe how you might help a student or a group of students understand the problem situation.

11. Watch clip 6.5, "Math Story Time." What did you notice about different children's mathematical thinking? How might you have responded in this situation?

CLIP 6.5 Math story time
http://hein.pub/YCM6.5

References

Carpenter, T. P., E. Ansell, M. L. Franke, E. Fennema, and L. Weisbeck. 1993. "Models of Problem Solving: A Study of Kindergarten Children's Problem-Solving Processes." *Journal for Research in Mathematics Education* 24 (5): 428–41.

Carpenter, T. P., E. Fennema, M. L. Franke, S. B. Empson, and L. W. Levi. 2015. *Children's Mathematics: Cognitively Guided Instruction*, 2nd ed. Portsmouth, NH: Heinemann.

7

Responding to Young Children's Mathematical Thinking

Eliciting and responding to children's mathematical ideas is central to supporting student learning. The earlier chapters provide a range of examples that highlight what you may see or hear from young children as they work to make sense of counting and problem solving. This chapter focuses on how you might respond to children's thinking to help them develop their mathematical ideas. Supporting and extending children's thinking can take many forms, but it begins with attending to the details of a child's existing understanding.

Starting with What Children Know and Can Do

Noticing the details of a child's thinking allows you to look beyond what they are not yet able to do and instead to focus on what they *can* do. As a teacher you probably would not expect each child in your classroom to begin the year able to accurately apply each of the counting principles discussed in Chapter 2, or to solve all of the kinds of problems detailed in Chapters 4, 5, and 6. But engaging children in counting and problem solving can allow each child to show what they know and can allow you as a teacher to use these existing understandings as a starting point. Consider how Tiana works to count a set of 5 jumbo crayons, and how her teacher Ms. Kern recognizes and acknowledges what Tiana is able to do.

> **Tiana:** *1, 4, 5, 2, 2.*
>
> **Ms. K:** *How many crayons do you have, Tiana?*
>
> **Tiana:** [counts again] *1, 2, 5, 2, 3.*
>
> **Ms. K:** *So how many crayons are in your collection?*
>
> **Tiana:** *2.*
>
> **Ms. K:** *I noticed that you pointed to each crayon as you counted! That's helpful when counting. Let's count them again together. You can point as we count.*

It would be easy to conclude that Tiana does not yet know how to count a set of 5 objects. However, Ms. Kern noticed that although Tiana was still working on learning the counting sequence and understanding that the last number assigned tells the amount in the set, she *did* point to each crayon as she counted, using exactly one number word for each object. Noticing this allowed Ms. Kern to explicitly recognize Tiana's competence and to choose a follow-up move that preserved Tiana's ownership of one-to-one correspondence and enabled her to use this knowledge to support her development of the other counting principles. Helping Tiana to see herself as successful not only supports her to continue to learn mathematics, it helps her to see herself as someone who has worthwhile mathematical ideas and to see mathematics as a place where her ideas matter.

Supporting Counting in the Moment

The following examples illustrate how teachers have used understanding of the mathematical principles that underpin learning to count, the ways that children begin to solve problems by modeling the actions and relations in the story, and the increasingly sophisticated ways that children's strategies develop over time to inform their instructional decision-making. In the first three examples, Ms. Romo is working with students in a small group as they count collections. She observes and elicits her students' strategies for counting and responds in a variety of ways. As the examples will show, Ms. Romo's in-the-moment instructional decisions are driven by her understanding of the details of individual students' thinking in relation to the counting principles.

Learning the Counting Sequence: Guadalupe

Guadalupe is counting a collection of 7 colored plastic spoons. She has arranged them into a row and counted them, touching each one as she counts.

> **Ms. R:** *How many spoons did you have, Guadalupe?*
>
> **Guadalupe:** *6.*
>
> **Ms. R:** *6? Can you show me how you counted?*
>
> **Guadalupe:** *1, 2, 4, 5, 4, 5, 6.*
>
> **Ms. R:** *Ah, I see. You touched each one as you counted, didn't you?* [smiles] *Let's see how many there are if you count my way.*
>
> **Ms. R and Guadalupe:** [slowly, touching 1 spoon with each number] *1, 2, 3, 4, 5, 6, 7.*
>
> **Ms. R:** *So how many spoons are in your collection?*
>
> **Guadalupe:** *7!*

In this example, Ms. Romo supported Guadalupe to extend her understanding of the counting sequence in ways that were linked with Guadalupe's demonstrated understandings of counting principles. Though she arrived at an incorrect total count, Guadalupe used exactly one number word for each object (one-to-one correspondence) and assigned an amount to the set based on the last number used in her count (application of the cardinal principle). Guadalupe knew a lot about counting; she demonstrated the accurate application of both one-to-one correspondence and the cardinal principle. She was still learning the conventional sequence of number names. Ms. Romo responded by first recognizing the competence that

Guadalupe displayed, and then scaffolding her use of the conventional counting sequence. Ms. Romo's final question served both to check back with the child to see if she understood the new counting sequence and to provide an opportunity for Guadalupe to once again demonstrate her understanding of the cardinal principle in naming the set.

Supporting One-to-One Correspondence: Marcus

Ms. Romo then turns to Marcus, who is working with a collection of 12 milk caps. The milk caps are lying on the table in an unorganized arrangement.

Ms. R: *How many milk caps do you have, Marcus?*

Marcus: [counts quickly out loud while pointing indiscriminately and hovering above the pile] *1, 2, 3, 4, 5, 6, 7, 8, 9, 10.*

Ms. R: *Oh wow, that was really fast. Can you slow down for me?*

Marcus: *1, 2, 3, 4, 5, 6, 7, 8, 9, 10, 11, 12, 13, 14, 15* [touches a cap inconsistently with each count; double-counts a few of the caps].

Ms. R: *Wow, Marcus, you can count really high. So do you think you have 10 or 15?*

Marcus: *I don't know.*

Ms. R: *Well, what could we do to figure it out?*

Marcus: *Count again? 1, 2, 3, 4, 5, 6, 7, 8, 9, 10, 11* [this time he has missed 1 cap]. *Hmm.*

Ms. R: *What do you think?*

Marcus: *I keep getting a different number.*

Ms. R: *Do you want to hand them to me as you count?*

Marcus: *Okay. 1, 2, 3, 4, 5, 6, 7, 8, 9, 10, 11, 12* [counts slowly and hands exactly 1 cap to his teacher with each count]. *12!*

Ms. R: *Are you sure?*

Marcus: *Yes, there's 12.*

Ms. R: *How do you know?*

Marcus: *I went slow and made sure that I counted each one, one at a time.*

Here Ms. Romo leveraged Marcus' understanding of the counting sequence with his emerging understanding of one-to-one correspondence. She first provided him with several opportunities to coordinate his counting sequence with each object, encouraging him by recognizing his ability to orally count accurately to 15. She then created space for him to think about why he might be getting different amounts, only introducing the idea of handing the caps to her when Marcus recognized that he was arriving at different amounts with each count. Her questions "Are you sure?" and "How do you know?" returned responsibility for sense making and ownership of the idea to Marcus and encouraged him to be explicit about his answer and what he has done that allowed him to be confident his answer was correct.

Supporting a Beginning Counter: Alex

Following this interaction, Ms. Romo turns her attention to Alex, who is counting a collection of 8 small rocks.

Ms. R: *Alex, did you count your rocks?*

[Alex points at a rock but does not count.]

Ms. R: *Can you count them for me?*

Alex: *1, 2, 3, 4, 5, 6* [touches each rock but oral count does not align with touching the rocks].

Ms. R: *So how many do you have?*

Alex: *1, 2, 3, 4, 5, 6, 9.*

Ms. R: *How many?*

Alex: *1, 2, 3, 4, 5, 6, 9, 10.*

Ms. R: *Ah, I see. I wonder . . . hmm.* [pauses] *If I wanted to have 3 rocks, could you give me 3 of your rocks?*

[Alex picks up 3 rocks in his hand and offers them to his teacher. Ms. Romo holds out her hand to accept the rocks and Alex dumps them into her hand.]

Ms. R: *How many did you give me?* [holding her hand open so that he can see the rocks he has given her]

Alex: *3.*

Ms. R: *You gave me 3 rocks. Thank you, Alex.*

In this interchange, we see that Alex is still developing his partial understandings of the counting principles. He used a fixed sequence of number names, but left out the numbers 7 and 8. He also demonstrated some one-to-one correspondence when counting, but did not seem to understand that the number he assigned to the last object tells him the total amount in the set, and instead recounted when asked how many he had. Seeing this, Ms. Romo made an intentional decision to support his development of the cardinal principle. She did this by first asking him to create a small set of 3 (an amount that could either be counted or subitized). After Alex successfully created this amount, his teacher reinforced his learning by repeating that *three* names the entire set ("You gave me 3 rocks").

There are many potentially productive ways Ms. Romo could have intervened to support Alex's learning of how to count. What is important to note about her decision-making here is that Ms. Romo intentionally modified the task (counting 8 rocks) to allow Alex to work with a smaller set that would support him to engage with the cardinal principle. In this way Ms. Romo's understanding of the counting principles, and her attention to the details of Alex's counting, allowed her to respond in a way that supported Alex to extend his understanding of cardinality while building from what he was already able do (count accurately to 5).

Deciding How Much to Intervene: Gus

Supporting the development of children's mathematical thinking involves not only providing in-the-moment support that is specific to a child's understandings, but also scaffolding in ways that allow children to take ownership of their learning. In the following example, Ms. Chan supports a child to extend his learning of the conventional counting sequence. In the situation described, Ms. Chan's preschoolers have entered the classroom after outside time and are lined up at the sink to wash their hands. Each child washes their hands for 20 seconds, keeping track of the time by counting out loud to 20. The numerals 1–20 are posted on the wall behind the sink for students to refer to if they wish. Ms. Chan listens carefully as each student

Teacher Reflection

In working through together how to support children as they counted, a group of preschool teachers brainstormed a variety of ways they could respond. Rather than settling on a single best response, they instead decided to list the different ways they could respond, recognizing that the decision they would make would depend on the child, the child's thinking, and the situation they were in. The teachers listed a number of options they had as they made decisions:

- Let it pass for now and come back to it later.
- Step in and do it correctly with the child.
- Ask the student a question (not a telling question, but rather a question about something the child has done).
- Highlight something the child has done correctly.
- Provide a tool (e.g., a container).
- Change or adapt the task (e.g., count a smaller collection, count only the blue ones).

recites the number sequence, providing support as necessary. For instance, as Gus's count crosses 10 his counting becomes tentative, and Ms. Chan begins to echo his count:

Gus: *eight, nine, ten,* [pauses] *eleven* [pauses] twelve.

Ms. C: *twelve.*

Gus: *furteen.*

Ms. C: *thirteen.*

Gus: *fourteen.*

Ms. C: *fourteen.*

[Gus pauses.]

Ms. C: *fif . . .*

Gus: *fifteen* [pauses] *sixteen.*

Ms. C: *sixteen.*

Gus: *seventeen.*

[Ms. C stops counting.]

Gus: *eighteen, nineteen, twenty!*

Ms. Chan let Gus take the lead in initiating the next number in the counting sequence and supported his learning by echoing his count. She listened closely to Gus's count, only providing the beginning sounds of the next number when Gus demonstrated that he needed assistance. She then backed off when Gus demonstrated he was able to finish his count to 20 without additional support. Throughout this exchange, Ms. Chan attended to both Gus' oral count and his expression (while surveying the other goings-on in the classroom). In doing so, she drew on her knowledge of Gus's thinking; she knew from previous observations that he often skipped 15, and used this to strategically vary her support of his learning of the counting sequence.

Supporting Children to Extend Counting into Problem Solving

Just because children are still developing their ability to accurately apply and coordinate the fundamental counting principles does not mean that they cannot begin to attempt to solve problems. As we saw in Chapters 4 and 6, children can model the actions or relations within problem situations as they are still learning to count.

Problem Solving with Emerging Counting: Jasmine

Consider how Ms. Villalpando capitalizes on the opportunity for Jasmine to engage in problem solving even when her counting of her collection is not completely accurate.

Jasmine works to count a collection of 14 colored popsicle sticks. There are 5 blue, 4 red, 3 yellow, and 2 green popsicle sticks. She has organized her popsicle sticks by color.

> **Jasmine:** [counts out loud, touching each popsicle stick] *1, 2, 3, 4, 5, 6, 7, 8, 9, 10, 11, 12, 14, 17.*
>
> **Ms. V:** *How many do you have?*
>
> **Jasmine:** *17.*
>
> **Ms. V:** *Interesting. What if you gave all of the red ones to me?*
>
> **Jasmine:** [slides the 4 red popsicle sticks over to her teacher, then counts the remaining sticks] *1, 2, 3, 4, 5, 6, 7, 8, 9, 10.*
>
> **Ms. V:** *So how many popsicle sticks do you have now?*
>
> **Jasmine:** *10. And you have 4!*

In Jasmine's first count, we learned that she, like many young children, was still working on learning the number names in the teens. Ms. Villalpando recognized this, but made a decision not to address this challenge today and instead engaged Jasmine in a problem situation offered by the context of the collection of colored popsicle sticks. Although on this day Jasmine was not able to accurately count her collection of 14 objects, she was able to solve a Separate (Result Unknown) problem by first modeling the action in the story, then using her ability to accurately count to 10 to provide a correct answer. Even if she were to have made an error in counting her remaining sticks, opportunities to engage in problem solving like this one provide a way for Jasmine to link her emerging understanding of counting with her intuitive sense of mathematical operations.

Understanding the Story: Isaac

Attending to the details of what children do to solve problems and understanding how children are likely to begin allow teachers to support children to make sense of problem situations and to develop strategies for themselves. Ms. Farrar has posed the following problem to her class of kindergarteners.

> *Brianna and her friends are playing hide and seek. Some children are hiding behind the curtain, but Brianna can still see their shoes. If there are 5 children hiding behind the curtain, and each child is wearing 2 shoes, how many shoes can Brianna see?*

As children are working on solving the problem, Ms. Farrar notices that Isaac has drawn 5 circles, then 2 circles, and written the numeral 7 (see Figure 7.1) on his paper. She asks him about the 7 he has written, and Isaac explains that he counted the 5, and then the 2 more, and that was 7.

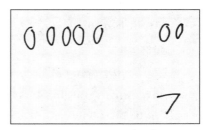

Figure 7.1 Isaac's initial solution

> **Ms. F:** *Oh, I see. So, Isaac, what's our story about?*
>
> **Isaac:** *Hide and seek.*
>
> **Ms. F:** *Mm hmm. And what else?*
>
> **Isaac:** *5 childrens.*
>
> **Ms. F:** *Yep. And what are the 5 children doing?*

Isaac: *They're hiding.*

Ms. F: *Okay. Anything else?*

Isaac: *There's 2 more.*

Ms. F: *Yes, you're right—there is a 2 in the story. Shall we see what that 2 is all about?* [rereads story]

Ms. F: *So, Isaac, what do these* [points to the 5 circles on his paper] *mean in our story?*

Isaac: *The 5 childrens who are hiding.*

Ms. F: *So how many shoes is this child wearing?* [points to the first circle]

Isaac: *2. Oh!*

Ms. F: *Does that make sense?*

[Isaac nods and begins to draw two lines inside of each circle. Ms. Farrar stands and observes Isaac for another moment, then walks away.]

Prior to posing the day's problem, Ms. Farrar anticipated that some students might approach the problem as Isaac did, possibly because the class had previously solved and shared strategies for several problems where the children were joining two quantities in the story. After asking about what Isaac had done, Ms. Farrar first tried to find out what Isaac understood about the story. From his responses Ms. Farrar interpreted that he had made sense of the 5 children playing hide and seek, but that what the 2 represented in the story was unclear to him; Isaac might have been thinking that the story was about 2 more children joining the 5 children hiding behind the curtain. With this in mind, Ms. Farrar revisited the story and asked Isaac about a part of his existing strategy that showed understanding (the 5 circles). Following this, she asked a specific question about something that Isaac had written (the first circle) in relation to the story (the shoes that a single child would be wearing). This supported Isaac to reinterpret the story as a situation involving 5 groups of 2, which allowed him to revise his existing strategy. In checking in with Isaac, Ms. Farrar supported him to attend to what he knew about the story in relation to his strategy.

Providing a Challenge: Xitlaly

At another table, Xitlaly has written a *10* on her paper. Ms. Farrar approaches and asks Xitlaly to talk about what she has done.

Ms. F: *Can you tell me about what you did?*

Xitlaly: *I used my fingers.*

Ms. F: *Can you show me and tell me the numbers you said?*

Xitlaly: *2, 4, 6, 8, 10* [raises 1 finger with each count].

Ms. F: *Oh, I get it now. Can you write the numbers that you just said on your paper?*

Xitlaly: *Uh huh* [writes *2 4 6 8 10*].

Ms. F: *Great. Now I can see what you did by looking at your paper. So I have another story for you, okay?*

[Xitlaly nods.]

Ms. F: *So what if the kids who were hiding behind the curtain weren't wearing shoes, but they were barefoot? How many toes would 1 person have?*

Xitlaly: *5 on one foot and 5 on the other foot.*

Ms. F: *So what could you do to figure out how many toes would be showing if there were 5 children hiding behind the curtain?*

Xitlaly: *Use the cubes?*

Ms. F: *What would you do with the cubes?*

Xitlaly: *Make the toes?*

Ms. F: *Okay, do you want to try that?*

[Xitlaly counts out 5 cubes, then another 5.]

Ms. F: *So what have you done so far?*

Xitlaly: *I made 2 feet.*

Ms. F: *Okay, so how many people is that?*

Xitlaly: *1 person.*

Ms. F: *And how many people are hiding behind the curtain?*

Xitlaly: *5.*

Ms. F: *So what are you going to do next?*

Xitlaly: *Make the other feet.*

Ms. F: *Sounds like a plan* [walks away].

Throughout this exchange, Ms. Farrar responded in situationally specific ways that are directly related to Xitlaly's mathematical ideas. She began by asking Xitlaly a general question, and then followed up with a more specific question after Xitlaly's initial explanation did not make the details of her strategy clear. Ms. Farrar then encouraged Xitlaly to capture the details of her strategy by recording the specific numbers in her count. At this point, Xitlaly

Teacher Reflection

As a teacher, I appreciate the flexibility of Cognitively Guided Instruction—it is so easy to differentiate! I can support those who are still learning to understand problems or develop accurate counting strategies and challenge students who are itching to show off their knowledge of larger numbers.

—**Kelly Odell Schumacher,** *transitional kindergarten teacher*

had already solved, provided an explanation, and recorded her counting strategy, and there were many possible ways Ms. Farrar could extend Xitlaly's thinking. She could have asked questions to promote reflection on how the details of Xitlaly's strategy were connected to the quantities and relationship in the problem, supported Xitlaly to write a number sentence that matched her strategy, invited her to solve using another strategy or a different tool, or adapted the problem by increasing the number of children playing hide and seek (for more on teachers' supporting and extending moves, see the references and further reading at the end of the chapter). Ms. Farrar made a decision to extend Xitlaly's thinking by adapting the story context to pose a challenge problem. In particular, Ms. Farrar was curious if, having counted by twos for the initial problem, Xitlaly would solve the challenge problem by counting by fives or tens.

In posing the challenge problem, Ms. Farrar made several successive moves to support Xitlaly in making sense of the problem and to get started. First, she did not pose a brand-new problem, but rather adjusted the context slightly. She then asked a question ("How many toes would 1 person have?") to check that Xitlaly had made sense of the new problem context and to orient her to the new group size. Ms. Farrar then supported Xitlaly to get started with a strategy of her choosing and to reflect on her partial strategy in relation to the story situation. Once she was confident that Xitlaly had a way to get started, Ms. Farrar left Xitlaly to continue her strategy on her own.

Supporting Children to Create Their Own Problems

In many examples throughout this book, the teacher poses the mathematical problem. But children can and do regularly create their own problems. Supporting children to pose problems for themselves as they engage in play or other activities is mathematically productive and often leads to the creation of problems that children care about and understand.

One way to support children to create problems is to mathematize everyday activities. Teachers can engage children in talking about a situation and thinking about what might happen and the questions that could be asked. In the following example, Ms. Torres's class is eating grapes during snack. As they are eating, the children are informally talking about who likes grapes, who doesn't like grapes, and the other colors of grapes that they have seen before (today's grapes are green).

> **Jason:** *I have grapes.*
>
> **Ms. T:** *How many grapes do you have, Jason?*
>
> **Jason:** *1, 2, 3, 4, 5, 6. 6.*
>
> **Ms. T:** *Okay, you have 6 grapes. What story should we tell about your grapes? What could happen?*
>
> **Jason:** *I could eat them!*
>
> **Kendra:** *Your mom could give you some more.*
>
> **Jessica:** *They fall on the ground.*
>
> **Hakim:** *Share them.*
>
> **Ms. T:** *So many good ideas! What do want to have happen to the grapes in your story, Jason?*

Here Ms. Torres helped her students to begin to think about things that might happen to a set of grapes, which are linked with actions that can begin to develop informal understandings of mathematical operations. Even though they did not solve an entire problem, the children began to explore the actions of eating (taking away) and getting more (joining). Understanding these actions and how they affect quantities is at the core of the relationship between addition and subtraction. The children are seeing where story problems come from, that they are supposed to make sense, and that the actions have particular mathematical meaning. Ms. Torres also allowed the students themselves to begin to take on roles as problem posers—this supports them to see themselves as doers of mathematics who have a voice in deciding what is interesting or important mathematically.

Another way to engage children in making up problems is to involve them in a storytelling game. Someone begins by giving a context for the story, and successive children contribute what happens next. Sometimes a contribution to the story can be mathematical. For instance, the class can work together to tell a story about visiting Taye's house. The teacher might start the story by saying, "I walked up to the door and knocked 5 times (knock together 1, 2, 3, 4, 5). I waited until someone answered." She then passes it on and the child sitting next to her says, "Taye opens the door and they go to the backyard." The teacher could let the story continue or pause it and ask, "How many rooms did they walk through to get to the backyard?" The next child continuing the story says in the backyard they played on the swings. The teacher could ask what else the child sees. A child might say, "I see 5 chairs." The teacher again could take this up and ask, "What would happen if we took 2 chairs away?" or she could continue the story. The game continues with children adding to the story. The children can solve and discuss each problem as it is posed before moving on to the next part of the story or they can tell the story without ever solving the problem that was posed. The act of telling the story and thinking about the numbers and the relationships they create supports children's sense making about math stories. At first you will need to help with the storytelling so that children can see how the story game works, but the goal is to let the children take over. Teachers can build on this work by posing problems with contexts that children choose or that are familiar to students, such as a book the class has read together, a student's personal interests, or practices outside of school.

Supporting Children to Represent Their Mathematical Thinking

Children are quite good at representing their ideas and can do so by showing on paper what they did. Children can begin to represent even as they count collections. Supporting children to represent their count can start with asking them to show how they have counted their collection on paper. This can be done as a follow-up after children have already counted their collections, or posed at the beginning as part of the task of counting collections. Children are often eager to represent their collection in a variety of ways (tracing objects, making a small mark or circle for each object, writing the numerals that they are saying out loud, and so on). Recording how they have counted their collection can support children to develop ideas of mathematical representation while also reinforcing their coordination of the counting principles.

Teachers often find it is powerful to engage with children around their representation, both as they are working on recording their thinking and after they have completed their recording. They may ask children to describe their representation, to recount the representation they have created on paper, to connect the written marks to the physical objects, or to consider another child's representation. Consider how Ms. Gaxiola supports Jayleen to connect counting and representing her collection.

Jayleen has counted a collection of 6 large buttons. She has placed the buttons onto her paper, and drawn circles underneath each one (Figure 7.2). She taps her teacher on the shoulder to get her attention to show her what she has done.

Figure 7.2 Jayleen represents her collection of 6 buttons.

> **Ms. G:** *Did you put all of them?*
>
> [Jayleen nods.]
>
> **Ms. G:** [looking underneath the buttons] *Oh, did you match them?*

[Jayleen nods again.]

Ms. G: *Oh, you did. You matched each one* [slides the buttons off of the paper]. *How many do you have on your paper now?*

Jayleen: *5* [holds up 5 fingers].

Ms. G: *5? Can you count them?*

Jayleen: [points to and touches each circle on her paper] *1, 2, 3, 4, 5, 6.*

Ms. G: *How many do you have?*

Jayleen: *6.*

Ms. G: *6?*

[Jayleen nods yes.]

Ms. G: *Do you want to write the number 6?*

Jayleen: *Yes.*

[Ms. Gaxiola then helps Jayleen to write the numeral 6 on her paper.]

In this example, recording Jayleen's collection has supported her to work on creating a mathematical representation, as well as to reinforce her understanding of one-to-one correspondence. First, Jayleen is beginning to attach a physical object (button) to a mark on her paper (a circle). This idea of abstracting a real-life object into a mathematical representation feeds into a big mathematical idea—that you can use tools to represent quantities, which can then be used to solve problems. (Children often intuitively apply this idea when they use their fingers to represent some other quantity, such as their age or how many blueberries they want to eat.) In this example, Jayleen's teacher supported her to connect a mathematical representation, 6 circles, with another representation, the numeral 6. Finally, Ms. Gaxiola used Jayleen's representation as a way to have her reflect on the total amount in her collection. Jayleen's strategy of "matching" each button to a circle, and her teacher's prompt to then re-count the circles, provided Jayleen with another opportunity to develop one-to-one correspondence. In this case, it also served as a check on her answer to the question of how many buttons she has in her collection.

Conclusion: Centering Children's Thinking in Instruction

Teaching and learning in real classrooms is messy. In our collective experience, early childhood teachers are immensely skilled in identifying and building from the kernels of productivity in children's words and ideas. Understanding the development of children's thinking and attending to the details of what children do can allow you to build from your strengths as an educator of young children. Recognizing and building from the potential that lies within children's informal, partial, or incomplete understandings can help children to see themselves as knowers and doers of mathematics and see school as a place where they can use their own ideas.

No one knows your students better than you. Attending and responding to the details of children's counting and problem solving allows you to notice each child's existing competencies and to use these as starting points to make decisions that support continued learning. As you gain experience in using children's thinking in your classroom practice, you will find that you are able to innovate and adapt your instructional materials and tasks to respond to what you have learned about your students' mathematical understandings. We have provided some examples of teachers doing this in Chapter 5, but you can begin to learn about your students' thinking by simply creating or recognizing opportunities to listen to and observe children as they engage in mathematics. There is no one way to make use of children's thinking in your classroom practice. What is important is that you find ways to learn about your students' thinking in ways that work and make sense for you. It can also be immensely valuable to engage in this work with your colleagues. Learning to use children's thinking is a journey. Getting started in some way, *any* way, will allow you to learn about and become curious about your students' rich intuitive mathematical ideas.

Questions for Further Reflection

1. This chapter opens with the idea that responding to children's thinking can be supported by focusing first on what children *can* do. Invite a young child who is just beginning to learn to count to count a small set of objects with you. What does this child already know about counting?

2. As you are with students during snack or breakfast, pose a problem to them related to what they are eating or talking about together. Prompt them to tell you how they solved the problem. Try a follow-up question that takes up something they said and ask them about it (e.g., "You said you used your fingers, can you show me what you did with them?").

3. Reread the interaction between Alex and Ms. Romo on p. 102. In this example Ms. R makes a decision to modify the task to develop Alex's understanding of the cardinal principle. What if instead she decided to intervene to support Alex's understanding of the number sequence or of the one-to-one principle? How might she have responded?

4. Reread the interaction between Xitlaly and Ms. Farrar on p. 107. In this example, Ms. Farrar decided to extend Xitlaly's thinking by adapting the story context to pose a challenge problem. What if instead she had decided to extend Xitlaly's thinking by inviting her to write a number sentence to go with her first strategy, or by adjusting one of the numbers in the story? What are some different number sentences that would match her strategy? How would you adjust the numbers in the story to provide different possible challenges?

5. What might be some opportunities within your classroom where children could begin to think about posing their own problems? Think about a photo or video that could offer opportunities to notice something mathematical. What do you think students would wonder about? What questions might they ask?

References and Further Reading

This chapter was greatly influenced by research that has examined the ways teachers support learning through eliciting the details of children's ideas and drawing on their knowledge of the development of children's thinking.

Empson, S. B., and V. R. Jacobs. 2008. "Learning to Listen to Children's Mathematics." In *Tools and Processes in Mathematics Teacher Education*, edited by D. Tirosh and T. Wood, 257–81. Rotterdam, The Netherlands: Sense Publishers.

Franke, Megan L., Angela C. Turrou, Noreen M. Webb, Marsha Ing, Jacqueline Wong, Nami Shin, and Cecilia Fernandez. 2015. "Student Engagement with Others' Mathematical Ideas: The Role of Teacher Invitation and Support Moves." *The Elementary School Journal* 116 (1): 126–48.

Jacobs, Victoria R., and Rebecca C. Ambrose. 2008. "Making the Most of Story Problems." *Teaching Children Mathematics* 15 (5): 260–66.

Jacobs, Victoria R., and Randolph A. Philipp. 2010. "Supporting Children's Problem Solving." *Teaching Children Mathematics* 17 (2): 98–105.

Kazemi, Elham. 2003. "Classroom Practices that Support Children's Mathematical Ideas." In *Teaching 4- to 8-Year Olds: Literacy, Math, Multiculturalism, and Classroom Community,* edited by C. Howes, 113–134. Baltimore, MD: Brookes.

8

Designing for Home–School Connections

So often young learners come into their first school experience and teachers expect them to fit into the school mold. I am trying to change my lens and look at what math knowledge children bring with them from home experiences. For example, when we play laundromat, do the children begin sorting clothes on their own? Do they pair socks? With intentional questioning, I learn what math experiences are happening at home or at the laundromat and I can plan to incorporate and expand upon these.

—Michelle Smith, prekindergarten teacher

In this chapter, we describe how you can identify and build on children's *multiple mathematical resources* to connect mathematics learning in and out of school and to validate practices and experience children bring from their homes and communities. We will highlight the mathematical practices children naturally engage with and challenge the notion that young children have limited mathematics experiences upon entering school. This is particularly important as children from cultural and linguistic backgrounds different from yours may engage in practices that may not immediately seem mathematical.

Children's Mathematical Resources

We have found that to provide children with culturally responsive math learning opportunities, it is important to draw on children's *multiple mathematical resources*. These resources include children's math thinking that we have discussed throughout this book, the ways they engage with math during play, and the resources they bring from their homes and communities. In this chapter we will focus on this last idea. Children have tremendous resources, and early childhood teachers, in particular, are very good at recognizing them. But sometimes there are resources that are not acknowledged either because historically they have not been considered a resource (e.g., multilingualism) or because the practices are sometimes unfamiliar to teachers.

The big ideas we hope you take from this chapter are:

- It is important to work *with* families to identify and honor home mathematical practices.
- Bridging home and family connections validates everyday practices and gives agency to families and children.
- The varied and diverse resources children have access to for supporting their mathematical learning might not always be evident.

We have organized the chapter with a series of vignettes to share what we have learned about how teachers notice, identify, and build on children's resources.

Informal Conversations: Julia's Robotics

To develop a reciprocal relationship with caregivers, Ms. Hanson always uses drop-off and pickup time to share something positive about what children have done in her Head Start classroom and asks the caregivers if they have seen a similar activity in the home. During a conversation with Julia's father at pickup time, Ms. Hanson learned that the interest she has shown in playing robot in the classroom is actually an interest in robotics and technology.

> Ms. Hanson shared with Julia's father that Julia has been very nice to a new child in the class and that the two enjoyed playing robot. She asked if Julia played robot at home like she did in school. The father shared that after watching a movie, Julia had told him that when she was bigger she was going to school to learn how to build robots. Later that week, Ms. Hanson asked Julia's grandmother about the robotics during drop-off. Julia's grandmother told Ms. Hanson that Julia loves tinkering to figure things out and that she buys small electronics from garage sales for Julia to take apart and put back together.

We often see teachers engage with caregivers during pickup and drop-off. Although that time is brief, there is opportunity to ask questions about what children have been doing at home, their favorite activity, or what the caregivers see as a particular strength. To do this in ways that caregivers are comfortable sharing, the teachers we work with make sure families understand why they are asking questions. If Ms. Hanson had not asked about playing robot at home, she might not have learned about Julia's interest or identified her skills in robotics as a resource. From these informal conversations with multiple caregivers that started with Julia's interest, Ms. Hanson was able get a better understanding of the resources—materials (electronics) and support (encouragement from her father and grandmother)—available to her. A teacher who learned about this interest could make sure there were many opportunities to build and rebuild things in the class. This would provide the chance to ask any number of counting questions such as "How many parts do you need?" or "How many parts have you used?" Julia's example has a lot of obvious mathematical connections but the reason Ms. Hanson learned about them was because she asked questions. Ms. Hanson provides us with an example of the importance of asking different questions to different people involved in children's lives. Even an example as powerful as Julia's with so much mathematics might be missed if you do not ask the right questions.

Conferences: Jana and the Antique Cars

Ms. Davis uses family–teacher conferences as a time not only to share what the child is doing in school but also time for families to share about practices and experiences at home. In the classroom, Jana usually gravitates to the dramatic play area and Ms. Davis assumed her interest in dolls and playing house would be evident in her home.

> During her conference with Jana's mother, Ms. Davis shared that she often engages Jana in counting in the dramatic play area. Ms. Davis said that during those times, she found that Jana could count up to 10 as she set dishes on the table. She then asked if there were ways that Jana engaged with number at home. Jana's mom laughed and said that Jana doesn't ever play house at home and grumbles when she is asked to help in the kitchen. She said that Jana's favorite thing to do was help her father who is a mechanic and restores old cars. The family regularly goes to antique car shows and Jana can identify the make, model, and year of many cars. Jana knew that a 1978 model was older than a 1984 model.

Although Jana had not demonstrated the ability to count past 10 in the class, she recognized at some level that 1984 was greater than 1978. Jana's knowledge of cars and interest in car shows was an important resource that Ms. Davis was able to use to support Jana in learning to count. Ms. Davis brought in some old matchbox cars and invited Jana to play car show. Jana organized the cars in rows and they worked together to count the cars. This became a regular activity that other children joined as Jana explained to them about the kinds of cars and what happens at a car show.

Home Visits: Iliana's Calendar

Over the course of the year, Ms. Murphy tries to do a home visit with most of her students' families. When she originally contacted Iliana's mother about doing a home visit, she was invited to the family gathering at a local fast food chain.

> At the get-together, Ms. Murphy learned that Iliana's brother and sister live with a different family and the two families meet once a month for a family get-together at a location that gives the young children space to play. Ms. Murphy

talked with Iliana's mother and the adoptive mother of the other children as they watched the children play. Iliana's mom explained that Iliana really looks forward to these visits and keeps track of how long it will be before the next one and knows how long the visits will last.

As she thought about Iliana's relationships with her siblings and how important the family visits were, Ms. Murphy started thinking about the many children in her class who have a variety of family structures that may include different visitation schedules and how those schedules were a resource for their mathematics learning. Ms. Murphy got Iliana a calendar and wrote down when the next visit would be. Every day they counted how many days were left until the next visit.

Family Rituals: Eduardo's Stories

Mr. Altos teaches in a bilingual (Spanish and English) preschool. In advance of a home visit to Eduardo's family, Mr. Altos prepared a list of questions about the family's routines and Eduardo's parents' own schooling experiences.

During the visit, Mr. Altos learned that there are three languages spoken in the home—one of Eduardo's mothers is from Mozambique and speaks Portuguese and his other mother is from Cuba and speaks Spanish, and they both speak English as a second language. Mr. Altos also learned that oral storytelling is an important part of the family practice. Every night before bed, one of Eduardo's moms shares a story about her home country or her travel to the United States. During the stories they look at a map of the world to see where the stories take place.

Both multilingualism and oral storytelling (understanding beginning, middle, and end) are a resource for children's temporal organization. Mr. Altos had never met one of Eduardo's mothers and did not know that Eduardo also spoke Portuguese. These stories that Eduardo's mothers told, both the practice and the content, provide Eduardo with a rich understanding of different cultural practices, geographic distance, and time. Mr. Altos recognized Eduardo's understanding of story structure as providing a solid foundation for solving story problems. He also made connections to Eduardo's home stories when he posed story problems by having stories take place in Cuba and Mozambique.

Using Pop Culture: Dean and Skylanders™

Ms. Brewer had read an article about building on children's interest in popular culture as a fruitful way to bridge home and school (Hedges 2011). Dean was very quiet in the classroom and never shared what he did at home, so she made sure to ask about it during a home visit.

> Ms. Brewer met with Dean's mother and father at their home after school one day. During their conversation, Dean brought out a large bowl of the characters from the Skylanders video game and told Ms. Brewer the name of each one. Dean's parents also shared that the family regularly counted things in the house and outdoors; they knew from a recent visit to a restaurant when he was counting his French fries that Dean could count to at least 10. Prior to the home visit, Ms. Brewer had struggled to engage Dean in counting at all. She knew that a district wide kindergarten readiness assessment was coming and that he was not likely to demonstrate his counting skills in a formal interview. So, Ms. Brewer cut up a poster of Skylanders characters to make a deck of cards, or collection, for Dean to count and organize.

Ms. Brewer recognized Dean's interest in Skylanders was a resource she could build on to support Dean to count at school. We have seen several examples of children showing success in counting things when they are things the children care about or have interest in. By counting things that matter, children see the activity as sensible.

Family Games: Dhavan and the Tiger Game

Ms. Surry was planning materials for a family math night and decided to include some games from the different countries represented in her class. She knew that Dhavan's family recently had spent a month in India with family.

> During a home visit, Ms. Surry asked Dhavan's father about the kinds of games the children played on their visit. He described a game called Tiger in the Village and worked with Ms. Surry to modify the game for an upcoming family math night. In the game, each of the four corners of the classroom is a city in India— Mumbai, Delhi, Kolkata, and Yenragudem. The game begins with all of the children holding hands in a circle dancing to Indian music. When the music stops, the children run to any of the four cities and "hide" from the tiger, who was

played by Dhavan. When the tiger comes to a particular city, all of the children who fled to that city are out of the game. The children who are still in the game then go back to the circle, dance to the music, and flee to a city of their choice again when the music stops. This continues until all but the last child is caught by the tiger. That child is free!

After family math night, the game became a regular part of Ms. Surry's class. She paused to ask questions throughout—How many children did the tiger catch? Were there more or fewer children in Mumbai or Kolkata? Are there more children "in" the game now or "out" of the game? What strategies might give a child the most turns as Tiger? We find the last question particularly interesting and a different way to have children think about their counting. In playing the Tiger game, a child might make strategic choices to pick the smallest group in order to remain the tiger or to pick the largest group to let a friend get a chance at playing tiger. Because Dhavan played this game with his family, there are probably strategies he uses to achieve his goal—by asking about those strategies, Ms. Surry connects counting to a game the child plays at home.

Being Aware of Assumptions: Malia's Brownies

Sometimes story problems posed by adults or curricular materials are interpreted differently by children. Children often have had varied experiences with a given story situation. In other cases, problems may contain implicit assumptions or constraints that are not clear to children. Consider the following problem that was posed in Ms. Uhe's classroom.

> *3 children are going to share 9 brownies so that each child gets the same amount. How many brownies will each child get?*

There are at least two different assumptions within this problem. One is explicitly stated—that each child will get the same amount. However, there is also an implicit assumption that the children will share *all* of the brownies. When this problem was posed to Malia, she gave each child 1 brownie, but did not distribute the others (see Figure 8.1). When asked why, Malia explained that she was never allowed to have more than 1 brownie at a time, so the rest would have to be put into the refrigerator.

Figure 8.1 Sharing brownies

When asked what she could do if she wanted to share *all* of the brownies, Malia easily saw that she could continue to pass out brownies, but this was not her initial understanding of the story. Malia helps us to see how children draw on their life experiences in making sense of problems, and that they may do so in ways that are different from what we expect, but are still equally valid. We also see how the teacher's decision to ask Malia about her thinking created an opportunity to view Malia's strategy in relation to her home practices and allowed her teacher to see the underlying logic in Malia's reasoning.

Children's Resources for Learning Mathematics

Children's experiences in their homes and communities provide many rich opportunities to engage in mathematics, particularly activities involving counting and number. But beyond what might be considered typical mathematical activities, there are many resources that support children as they engage with mathematics both in and out of school. When people think about resources, they often view the idea from their own cultural experiences. For example, for someone who grew up in a family that played a lot of board games, it might be easy to assume that many families did the same thing and therefore most children had similar mathematical experiences. Imagining the unfamiliar and seeing rich resources in difference is not easy to do. In the stories above, we see examples of children's resources for learning mathematics that the teachers did not expect or initially were not aware of. Some of those resources come from things children are interested in doing such as Julia's tinkering, Jana's cars shows, or Dean's Skylanders. Some resources come out of family practices such as Iliana's monthly family gatherings, Eduardo's family stories, or Dhavan's tiger game.

Often, when people think of *resources*, they are thinking of particular things that might support learning, including physical objects such as books, computers, or games, and personal interactions such as encouragement to count things like steps as one climbs or the forks as one sets the table. Although we recognize the value in these ideas, they can limit our view of the wealth of other resources and therefore lead us to make assumptions about children's learning opportunities. The earlier examples show a broader way of thinking about resources by recognizing that all families provide experiences and things that serve to support children's mathematical thinking.

We also think it is important to consider how many practices and experiences in children's homes develop resources that the children can then use to do mathematics—these practices might not necessarily be directly tied to counting or problem solving but they are strengths that children bring and draw on when they are counting or solving problems. We tend to underestimate the ways children are learning to be independent, which might encourage us to provide more support than they need when solving problems or counting independently. For example, caring for siblings or helping with household chores can support the development of a sense of responsibility.

Identifying Children's Resources

There are many ways to learn about the resources children have available in their homes and communities. In the stories above, teachers used different opportunities to find out about children's lives outside of school. In all of these interactions, one of the key points is making the interaction reciprocal. By this we mean validating the *caregiver's* knowledge of a child rather than centering conversations on what the *teacher* knows about the child. By shifting the focus to what families know, those families see their role and experiences as critical contributions to the teacher's understanding of the child. In the home visit examples, the teachers went into the meeting with specific questions they wanted to ask about the child and family practices rather than focusing the conversation on the child's performance at school. The stories we share are but some of the many opportunities to learn about children's lives outside of school. In those situations when it is difficult to have contact with caregivers, listening to and observing children can provide insight into their interests and experiences.

Building on Children's Resources in the Classroom

In our work, we have found that teachers brought children's worlds into the classroom in multiple ways, ranging from drawing on children's practical expertise as they organize for instruction to integrating children's interests or replicating out-of-school experiences in the classroom. We've shared some of these in the previous examples. In addition, there are often other home or community practices that children engage with that teachers might bring into the classroom. Two examples we have seen based on home (or work) visits include converting the dramatic play area into a sandwich shop because a child spent his afternoons at the one where his parents worked, and a variety store, because a child went there daily with his mother. In both of these examples, the dramatic play area had multiple opportunities for children to engage in counting and problem solving.

Conclusion

We realize that teachers have many children in their classrooms and it can be challenging to imagine building on all of their interests. Furthermore, if an area is designed around the interests of one child, one might ask how that benefits other children. We find that a helpful way to think about this is using the metaphor of windows and mirrors. When one child's out-of-school experiences are evident in the classroom, that child sees their home reflected (as in a mirror) in the classroom, whereas other children have a window into that child's life. We saw that in the stories of Jana's car show and Dhavan's tiger game. The other children in these classes got to learn about their classmate's experiences, interests, and expertise.

The stories we have shared provide examples of how teachers opened up to new ideas of thinking about resources. They recognized varied and diverse resources for supporting children's mathematical learning that were not always evident and set aside their personal experiences and expectations to identify those resources.

They had to work hard to identify how resources might support learning, but most importantly, they worked *with* families to identify and honor home mathematical practices, which gave agency to families and children.

Questions for Further Reflection

1. This chapter offers some ideas for learning about children's interests and home experiences. How could you use or modify these ideas to fit your context? What are some other ways you might learn about children's interests and home experiences?

2. What are some questions that you might ask children or families to find out about their mathematical practices at home?

3. Think back on the example with Jana and the antique cars. What are some things about individual children in your class you could share during family conferences that might encourage caregivers to tell you about out-of-school experiences?

4. If you are able to do home visits, what questions might you ask? What information might you try to learn?

5. In the brownie example, Malia's solution reflects her reality. Think about the kinds of problems children in your class are asked to solve. How might their solutions differ depending on their real-life experience?

6. What if you were talking to a caregiver who shared that their child regularly counts to 20 but you have only seen the child count to 6 in your class? How would you respond? What questions would you ask the caregiver or the child?

References

A number of researchers have explored the ideas discussed in this chapter with respect to older students (particularly Lois Moll, Norma Gonzalez, and Marta

Civil's work on funds of knowledge). Specific references for their work and other readings follow.

Aguirre, J. M., E. E. Turner, T. G. Bartell, C. Kalinec-Craig, M. Q. Foote, A. Roth McDuffie, and C. Drake. 2013. "Making Connections in Practice: Developing Prospective Teachers' Capacities to Connect Children's Mathematical Thinking and Community Funds of Knowledge in Mathematics Instruction." *Journal of Teacher Education* 64 (2): 178–92. doi: 10.1177/0022487112466900.

Civil, M. 2002. "Everyday Mathematics, Mathematicians' Mathematics, and School Mathematics: Can We Bring Them Together?" In *Journal for Research in Mathematics Education: Everyday and Academic Mathematics in the Classroom*, edited by M. E. Brenner and J. N. Moschkovich, 40–62. Reston, VA: National Council of Teachers of Mathematics.

Foote, M. Q., A. Roth McDuffie, E. E. Turner, J. M. Aguirre, T. G. Bartell, and C. Drake. 2013. "Orientations of Prospective Teachers Towards Students' Families and Communities." *Teaching and Teacher Education* 35: 126–36.

González, N., L. C. Moll, and C. Amanti, eds. 2006. *Funds of Knowledge: Theorizing Practices in Households, Communities, and Classrooms*. London: Routledge.

Hedges, H. 2011. "Rethinking Sponge Bob and Ninja Turtles: Popular Culture as Funds of Knowledge for Curriculum Co-Construction." *Australasian Journal of Early Childhood* 36 (1): 25–29.

Turner, E. E., J. M. Aguirre, T. G. Bartell, C. Drake, M. Q. Foote, and A. Roth McDuffie. 2014. "Making Meaningful Connections with Mathematics and the Community: Lessons from Pre-Service Teachers." In *Embracing Resources of Children, Families, Communities, and Cultures in Mathematics Learning* [A Research Monograph of TODOS: Mathematics for ALL], Vol. 3, edited by T. G. Bartell and A. Flores, 30–49. San Bernardino, CA: TODOS.

9

Extending Counting to Develop Grouping and Base-Ten Understanding

In this chapter, we describe how you might extend children's counting experiences to develop their understanding of place value and the base-ten number system. In previous chapters, we have discussed the ways that counting collections of objects can support children to develop their understandings of the number sequence, one-to-one correspondence, and cardinality, as well as providing an opportunity to engage in problem solving. In this chapter, we will explore how engaging children in counting collections can support them to connect counting ideas with more sophisticated ideas of grouping: this is the foundation for understanding place value. It might seem curious that we address the development of base-ten understanding in a book focused on young children. It is our hope that by noticing the seeds of these ideas in what children do as they count, you will be better prepared to interpret their mathematical understanding and to decide when and how to respond in ways that build on children's intuitive sense making. We are not suggesting that early childhood teachers directly teach place value. Rather, our goal is to illustrate how ideas about the base-ten number system emerge naturally as children count.

The base-ten number system is built upon a recurring relationship between 10 groups of a unit and 1 group of another. For example, a group of 10 ones may be counted as 1 ten, a group of 10 tens can be counted as 1 hundred, and so on. Children can engage with these ideas through developing increasingly efficient strategies for counting their collections. We can see the seeds of these ideas emerge as young children intuitively sort objects into groups based on attributes. Over time, children will also begin to sort objects into groups with equal numbers of objects in each group. Eventually, children will begin to use these groupings to develop more sophisticated and efficient methods of counting. The ideas that emerge as children group objects and use these groupings to count provide opportunities for them to build understanding of the underlying structures that govern and give meaning to our base-ten number system. The development of these ideas will be elaborated on throughout this chapter.

Grouping Objects in a Collection

When counting collections, especially as collections become larger, children notice similarities and differences between objects in their collections and begin to sort their collections into groups based on a specific attribute, such as color or size (see Figure 9.1).

Although it might appear that a child is playing or not engaging in counting, sorting a collection into groups based on some common attribute can be thought of as a form of organizing for some children and may support them to be able to count larger quantities of objects because it subdivides the task of counting a larger collection into smaller subsets.

Figure 9.1 Counting pom poms after sorting by size

Some children may sort before counting their collection, after counting, or at the same time as they count.

For example, Jane is presented with a collection of 24 fruit pouch caps of various colors. Before counting, she creates piles of like colors, noting that she has more red pouch caps than any other color (Figure 9.2). She then proceeds to count her entire collection, but moves through the collection by successively counting all of the caps within each colored subset.

Figure 9.2 Fruit pouch caps sorted by color

> **Jane:** *1, 2, 3, 4, 5, 6, 7, 8, 9* [counts all the red caps], *10, 11, 12* [green], *13, 14, 15, 16* [orange], *17, 18, 19* [yellow], *20, 21, 22, 23, 24* [blue].

Counting a collection of this size is often challenging for young children because it can be difficult to keep track of which objects still need to be counted, but by sorting and organizing her collection into smaller groups by color, Jane only needed to make sure that she counted all of a single color before moving on to the next group.

Grouping Objects by Quantity

Sorting objects into groups by attributes lays a foundation for children to sort into equal groups based on quantity. Children may sort into groups that tend to be easier for them to skip count (such as twos, fives, or tens); they may sort into other sized groups (such as fours or sixes) that are not as easily skip counted. We refer to both kinds of groupings here. This method of grouping is significant for several reasons. First, grouping by quantity is a way that a child can impose an organizing attribute onto sets for which no clear differentiating physical attribute is apparent (e.g., a set of 30 wooden blocks). Second, because the child chooses to impose the group size themselves there are many possible ways to form groups for a given collection. When grouping by an attribute, the child is bound by the quantity of that attribute. So if counting by color, the quantity of each color is already present within the collection. But in grouping objects according to a given quantity, the child is able to decide on the size of the group. Third, grouping by quantity into equal groups makes it possible to create subsets within a collection that are new units themselves. This idea of "unitizing" a given quantity makes it possible to count a collection in multiple ways, using different aspects of the counting sequence.

Using Grouping to Skip Count

Consider Diego's grouping and counting strategies as he counts 20 small plastic cubes in Ms. Enriquez's class.

Diego: [sorts cubes into pairs, then counts] *2, 4, 6, 8, 10, 12, 14, 16, 18, 20.*

Ms. E: *Oh, nice. You grouped them by twos. Is there another way that you could group them?*

Diego: [rearranges cubes into groups of 5] *5, 10, 15, 20.*

Diego arranged his collection into groups of twos and then fives, which tend to be easier to skip count by.

Grouping and Counting by Ones

Many children may arrange a collection of objects into groups of equal size, but not yet be able to skip count, and will still need to count their collection by ones. In Ms. Gaxiola's class, Logan has organized his collection of 12 keys into 3 groups with 4 keys in each group.

Ms. G: *I see that you made some groups with your keys. Can you count them for me?*

Logan: *1, 2, 3, 4* [pauses, moves onto next group], *5, 6, 7, 8* [pauses], *9, 10, 11, 12.*

Ms. G: *How many keys did you have in your collection?*

Logan: *There's 12!*

Even though he has organized his collection into groups of 4, we would not expect for Logan, a preschooler, to skip count by fours in counting his whole collection. Still, he is beginning to develop ideas of equal groups even though this does not yet factor into how he counts his collection. It is not necessary for a child to be able to use equal groups to count for these groupings to be mathematically productive. It is also common that some children will begin to group objects by quantity without explicitly acknowledging, or being aware, that they are doing so. The more opportunities children are given to count a variety of collections, the more likely they will be to begin to group objects, and the more likely you will notice their intuitive ideas about grouping. You can then decide if and how you might build on their emerging understanding.

Base Ten and the Structure of the Number Sequence

Providing larger collections of objects for children to count can create opportunities for them to develop their understanding of the base-ten number system. As described in Chapter 2, the names of the numbers beyond 20 (within 100) are constructed by naming the decade and appending a recurring 1–9 sequence. This same idea governs how larger numbers are named (and written). 10 sets of ten are given the name "hundred," 10 hundreds are "one thousand," and so on.

Recall from Chapter 3 that many children begin to recognize this structure and employ it in some way as they attempt to count further into the counting sequence, even if they are not yet correctly counting the full sequence. Providing opportunities for children to count collections greater than 20 (even as they may still be struggling with the teens) can help them to engage with its underlying structure. In attempting to count further, children's emerging understanding of the base-ten number system is often revealed. Consider Maria's counting sequence as she attempts to count a collection of 38 objects.

> **Maria:** *1, 2, 3, 4, 5, 6, 7, 8, 9, 10, 11, 12, 13, 14, 15, 16, 17, 18, 19, 20, 21, 22, 23, 24, 25, 26, 27, 28, 29, twenty-ten, twenty-eleven, twenty-twelve, twenty-thirteen, twenty-fourteen, twenty-fifteen, twenty-sixteen, twenty-seventeen, twenty-eighteen.*

Maria's count shows an emerging understanding of the structure of our number system. Once the sequence arrives at 20, she forms subsequent numbers by adding the word *twenty* to the previously used sequence of number names. Though she uses a nonstandard sequence of number names in the thirties, the count makes sense.

For example, she names her thirty-eighth object "twenty-eighteen"; 20 plus 18 is in fact 38!

Some children recognize the repeating structure of 0–9 and apply this as they extend their understanding of the number sequence into new decades. In the following example, Joshua is counting out loud as he waits for his friend to finish drinking water at the water fountain.

Joshua: *1, 2, 3, 4, 5, 6, 7, 8, 9, 10, 11, 12, 13, 14, 15, 16, 17, 18, 19, 20, 21, 22, 23, 24, 25, 26, 27, 28, 29, 40, 41, 42, 43, 44, 45, 46, 47, 48, 49, 60, 61, 62, 63, 64, 65 . . .*

Joshua's count shows that he understands that the counting sequence is extended by adding the name of each successive decade to the 1–9 sequence. However, his learning of the sequence of decades is still emerging, as he has skipped the thirties and fifties. We have found that children commonly skip these two particular decades, as the roots of 3 and 5 within these decade names are somewhat hidden (as compared with the *six* within *sixty* or the *eight* within *eighty*, which tend to be easier for children to notice).

CLIP 9.1 Christopher counts to 100
http://hein.pub/YCM9.1

The work these children are doing in making sense of the structure of the number system as they count shows that they are not simply making mistakes but that they are noting something about the structure of the number system. This sense making is important for supporting the understanding of place value. It can be helpful to point out what is correct about Joshua and Maria's count to support their sense making.

Grouping by Tens

Given experience and opportunity, children will begin to organize objects in their collections into groups of ten that will make finding the final count friendlier or more efficient. Although teachers can support this development by providing larger collections to count, or by providing tools and containers to help children organize their collection, children themselves will naturally choose to group objects by quantities that make the task of counting easier. The more often that students count larger collections, the more you'll notice that they start grouping by tens.

Ana and Shreen choose a collection of over 85 beads. They start counting the beads one at time but quickly decide it might be better to put them in cups. They decide to put 10 beads in each cup and start to count 1–10 as they are making their groups of 10. They fill 8 cups of 10 and have 5 beads left over, which they leave in a neat line outside of the last cup. They proceed to count together, pointing to each cup as they count:

Ana and Shreen: *10, 20, 30, 40, 50, 60, 70, 80* [slight pause], *81, 82, 83, 84, 85.*

Providing tools that allow children to group objects (such as cups, lunch trays, or ten-frames) may support students to make these connections. However, just because a child can place objects into groups of 10 and can skip count by tens does not necessarily mean that they understand how to coordinate these two things to be able to count a collection. For example, consider Byron's organization and subsequent count in Ms. Morrissey's class (see Figure 9.3).

Figure 9.3 Byron's groups of 10 straws

He has organized 63 straws into 6 groups of 10 and 1 group of 3. He begins skip counting by tens from 10 to 60, pointing to each of the groups of 10. Then he continues the sequence by tens as he points to the individual straws in the group of 3.

Byron: *10, 20, 30, 40, 50, 60, 70, 80, 90* [points to each of the groups of 10 and then the individual straws in the group of 3].

Ms. M: *Nice counting by tens, Byron. How many straws are in this pile* [points to sixth pile of 10]?

Byron: *10.*

Ms. M: *How about this pile?* [points to seventh pile, which contains only 3]

Byron: *3.*

Ms. M: *Hmm. So how many straws did you say you had?*

Byron: [counts again] *10, 20, 30, 40, 50, 60* [pauses], *61, 62, 63.*

Ms. M: *Okay, so do you have 90 or 63?*

Byron: *63. There isn't 10 in this last pile.*

In this example, Byron was quickly able to note his counting of 1 straw as 10 and to adjust accordingly. However, some children may not be as quick to recognize this and may persist in counting by tens for both groups of 10 and single objects or may place leftovers of less than 10 into a final group (e.g., 7), but count this final group as a 10.

While children often learn to count by tens (or rather, count the decade numbers), often to 100, they do not necessarily connect a rote count of tens with the idea that each count of 1 ten contains 10 ones. It is important to provide children with time and opportunity to develop an incentive to group objects and to make these connections, rather than telling students to group their objects into tens and count by tens because it's easier or more efficient. One of the ways teachers can support children to want to organize their collections into groups that will make counting easier is to provide opportunities for children to count larger and larger collections. For example, even if a child is able to count by tens, there is little incentive to apply this idea in counting a relatively small collection (of say, 14 items or even quantities in the 20s). This child would be much more likely to use their ability to group and count by tens if the collection were substantially larger (greater than 50, or even 100). Grouping by tens in a collection allows the child to see what the quantity looks like when they alternate between counting tens and ones—from counting 10, 20, 30 to 31, 32, 33 and so on. The collection is a context that makes sense to the child and supports them to engage in problem solving around counting different units.

CLIP 9.2 Daniel counts pennies and makes tens
http://hein.pub/YCM9.2

CLIP 9.3 Hector counts blocks and makes tens
http://hein.pub/YCM9.3

Building Relationships Between Tens and Hundreds

Ideas of grouping and counting by tens can be extended when children are given opportunities to count even larger collections (with more than 100 items). Colin and Lily are counting a collection of 232 bottle caps. They quickly start to count out piles of 10. Lily suggests that they should put 10 piles in a row and then begin a new row. Taking up her idea, the pair organizes their piles into rows of 10, finishing with a total of 23 piles of 10 and 4 extra bottle caps not in a pile. While Lily is neatly organizing the piles, Colin counts the piles by tens.

> **Colin:** *10, 20, 30, 40, 50, 60, 70, 80, 90, 100* [slight pause], *110, 120, 130, 140, 150, 160, 170, 180, 190, 200* [pause], *210, 220, 230, 234.*

Whereas Colin counts each individual group of 10 to arrive at his total, Lily makes use of the fact that the piles are in rows of 10 and her understanding that 10 tens is 100.

> **Lily:** *I know 10 tens is 100. So, 200* [pause], *230, 234.*

Colin has made use of his ability to count by tens well above 100 to count a very large collection and successfully navigated accurately counting by tens across 100 and 200 (two places children often experience difficulty). Lily, however, has regrouped her 23 groups of 10 into 2 groups of 10 tens, 3 more tens, with 4 leftover.

The careful reader will have also noticed that Colin and Lily were counting a collection of 232 bottle caps, not in fact the 234 that they arrived at with their final count. As is common when children count larger collections, they have made a small error in making their groups of 10, and two of their groups only contain 9 bottle caps each. It is certainly possible that if a teacher noticed this she might suggest that Colin and Lily double-check that each of their piles does in fact have 10. However, depending on the teacher's goal, it may be less important that children arrive at a completely accurate total in counting collections of this size. It may instead be the case that the

Teacher Reflection

Don't be afraid to give large collections to young children! They genuinely want to know how many there are in the collection. Counting larger collections allows children to think about how they want to count, how they organize the count, and how they keep track of how many they have counted. It reinforces that there are multiple ways to approach a task and allows children to work on building stamina and perseverance. As a teacher, I can listen in to understand where the child's threshold is and think about how to support them. Counting larger collections can be easily differentiated because if a child is struggling with the entire collection, I can pull a smaller portion from the collection and encourage them to start with that pile.

—**Darlene Fish Doto,** *teacher and elementary math specialist*

Teacher Reflection

I find many benefits in having my students count larger collections. Large collections allow students to recognize patterns in numbers and to hear those number sequences repeated. Students see that larger numbers aren't scary or impossible, and they have a sense of accomplishment when the task is completed. Students who may struggle counting by ones to 100 can still be successful counting a larger collection if they are proficient at counting by tens. Large collections can also promote efficiency in organization and counting. Students quickly find that counting a large collection by ones takes a long time and is cumbersome to record. Students also develop flexibility. One of the extensions I use in my classroom is to "count and organize in more than one way" with the same collection. For example, a student may organize a collection of 125 objects into 12 groups of 10 and 5 ones, and then reorganize their groups into 25 groups of 5, or 6 groups of 20 and 5 ones.

—**Wendy Moulton,** *kindergarten teacher*

teacher's primary goal in asking her students to count such a large collection is for them to engage in the process of deriving and executing a strategy that involves making many groups of objects and figuring out how to count a large number of groups. In this case, the teacher might exercise her professional judgment and decide that Colin and Lily's error in their total count here is a minor concern. She might instead focus on having the pair articulate and make sense of the relationships between their two counting strategies (and in doing so, continue to deepen their mathematical understanding of the place value knowledge and relationships embedded within their strategies).

Counting Packages of Items

As children's understanding of counting and grouping continues to develop, they may draw upon these ideas in the strategies that they devise to count more complicated collections. Teachers sometimes choose to support these opportunities by providing packages of items for students to count. For example, a collection might consist of wrapped sets of 2, 3, or 4 crayons (as are often given out to children at restaurants); packages of 9 erasers; boxes of 24 crayons; or decks of 52 cards. We have worked with teachers who have found asking students to inventory classroom supplies throughout the year to be an engaging way for students to count large sets of objects and for teachers to learn about their student's thinking when counting. This can be one way to provide children with opportunities to count collections that are composed both of packaged sets and of loose items. In these cases, teachers usually require that children leave the packages unopened to push them to use the set as a unit rather than as individual objects.

Counting packaged items complements students' experiences with grouping by quantities (see Figure 9.4). Working with individual item collections gives students the choice of how they want to group their collection; working with packaged collections provides a grouping structure already imposed on the collection (that is, the erasers are already in groups of 9). However, this does not mean that students must rigidly follow the package quantities. In developing strategies to count these larger collections that consist of predetermined sets of items, students will sometimes draw on their understanding of number composition and the base-ten number system. Consider how Sha'ron and Anita devise a method to count their collection of 5 boxes of 12 pencils.

Figure 9.4 Dynasty counts packages of 4 pencils by ones.

Sha'ron: *We could count by tens.*

Anita: *What? I don't get what you mean.*

Sha'ron: *Look. 10, 20, 30, 40, 50* [pointing to each of the 5 packages].

Anita: *But there's 12 in each.*

Sha'ron: *Right, so we have to count the rest of them.*

Anita: *Oh, so 2, 4, 6, 8, 10!* [pointing again to each of the 5 packages] *And 50 and 10 is 60. So there's 60!*

Children might draw upon their understandings of creating groups of single items to create groups that contain their packaged items in a collection. In the following example, Miles and Deion are counting a collection of markers that includes boxes with 8 markers to a box, as well as a large bag of loose markers. Being five- and six-year-olds, they struggle to count by eights, and as Ms. Gupta circulates, she notices that this pair seems stuck in coming up with an approach to counting their collection.

Ms. G: *I see that you've laid out your boxes of markers. Have you figured out how you're going to count up all of the markers?*

Miles: *We don't know how to count by eights.*

Ms. G: *Yeah, counting by eights can be tricky. Is there another number you can think of to count by?*

Miles: *I like counting by tens, but there are 8 in each box.*

Ms G: *Hmm* [pauses]. *I wonder if there's a way you can use your counting by tens here.*

Deion: [had been holding the bag of loose markers in his hand while Miles and Ms. Gupta were focusing on the boxes laid out] *Oh I know! Now there's 10!* [takes out 2 loose markers and puts them next to a box]

Miles: *What do you mean there's 10?*

Deion: *Look* [pointing to the box]. *8* [pause], *9, 10! We can make tens!*

Ms. Gupta then walked away, leaving the pair with space to figure out the rest of their collection. Miles and Deion continued to place 2 loose markers next to each box of 8 until they had formed groups of 10. They continued to make groups of 10 with the remaining loose markers and counted by tens to figure out their total.

Counting packaged collections allows children to build from their experiences counting collections of single objects and to extend their sense making to a more expansive number set. Children draw upon their number sense and base-ten understanding to come up with inventive and mathematically elegant strategies. There are many ways that children may count a given collection that contains packages of items. For instance, a collection of markers that includes boxes of 12 as well as single loose markers might be counted by ones, skip counted by twelves, decomposed into tens and twos and then counted, or even regrouped into twenty-fives by combining 2 twelves to make 24, and then adding a loose marker to make 25. The ways children choose to count are shaped by both their developing number sense and the specific amounts within a package.

Problem Solving with Groups of 10

The strategies students use when attempting to count items arranged into groups of 10 or premade packages in many ways parallel the strategies they use to solve story problems involving groups of 10. Recall in an earlier example how Byron arranged his straws into groups of 10 with 3 remaining straws. He counted 10, 20, 30, 40, 50, 60, 61, 62, 63.

Shortly thereafter, Byron was asked to solve the following problem.

> *For his birthday Byron got 4 packs of baseball cards. There are 10 baseball cards in each pack. He also got 7 more cards,*

which weren't in a pack. How many baseball cards did Byron get for his birthday?

Byron held out his hand and counted "10, 20, 30, 40," raising a finger with each count. He then paused and lowered his 4 fingers, and began counting again, raising a finger with each number spoken: "41, 42, 43, 44, 45, 46, 47. 47."

In both counting his collection and solving his problem, Byron engaged with core ideas of the base-ten system. The development of children's base-ten ideas is addressed more fully in *Children's Mathematics* (Chapter 6).

Conclusion

In this chapter, we have explored some of the ways that counting can be extended to support children to engage with increasingly sophisticated mathematical ideas. This development can follow from young children's intuitive ideas. Children's natural tendency to organize and group items in their collections can provide a foundation that can be built upon and extended into base-ten understanding. Creating opportunities for children to work with larger collections of objects can provide incentives for children to derive and apply increasingly complex counting and grouping strategies. In this way, very large collections of objects and packaged objects offer potential to help children make sense of very large quantities and to connect their understandings of these quantities with the mathematics that underpins place value, multiplication, and division.

Questions for Further Reflection

1. Invite a child you know to count a collection of objects that is large enough to be a bit beyond the child's understanding of the conventional counting sequence. Watch and listen to see what the child says and does when the number names become challenging. What does this child know about the counting sequence?

2. Sometimes teachers will make tools such as cups, bowls, trays, ten-frames, or hundreds charts available to their students as they are counting. What are some potential benefits of providing tools such as these? What are some potential drawbacks?

3. Look back at Figure 9.2, where Jane has sorted and then counted the collection of 24 colored fruit pouch caps. Recalling some of the ideas presented in Chapter 4, what follow-up questions could you ask that would provide an opportunity for Jane to engage in problem solving?

4. Reread the example in the chapter where Colin and Lily worked together to count 232 bottle caps. What questions could you ask the pair to help them to think about the relationship between their different ways of counting?

5. Consider the following problem that Byron solved near the end of the chapter:

For his birthday Byron got 4 packs of baseball cards. There are 10 baseball cards in each pack. He also got 7 more cards, which weren't in a pack. How many baseball cards did Byron get for his birthday?

What do you predict are the other ways that children might solve this problem? After predicting, pose this problem to several children. In what ways did their strategies match your predictions? What did you learn about these children's understanding of base-ten number concepts?

References and Further Reading

Carpenter, T. P., E. Fennema, M. L. Franke, L. Levi, and S. B. Empson. 2015. "Base-Ten Number Concepts." In *Children's Mathematics: Cognitively Guided Instruction*. 2nd ed., 84–95. Portsmouth, NH: Heinemann.

Jaslow, L. B., and V. R. Jacobs. 2009. "Helping Kindergarteners Make Sense of Numbers to 100." *The Journal of Mathematics and Science: Collaborative Explorations* 11: 195–213.

Schwerdtfeger, J. K., and A. Chan. 2007. "Counting Collections." *Teaching Children Mathematics* 13 (7): 356–61.

10

Conclusion:
Toward Coherence
and Understanding

Remember children are naturally limitless and so is mathematics. Remember each child is unique, and they have their own way of learning the concept that you are trying to teach. Be patient and easy on yourself, allow them to explore and build on their strengths and abilities.

—Dolores Torres, preschool teacher

I've been teaching as an early childhood educator for the past thirteen years and for the first time I feel like I have truly learned so much about mathematical skills as they develop at an early age. Working on counting collections with three- and four-year-old children has been enlightening, as I have learned to objectively observe and guide children appropriately. Children at this age have an innate ability to learn and understand. By engaging in counting collections, children were able to demonstrate and acquire mathematical skills. Children were able to use the counting sequence, develop one-to-one correspondence, demonstrate understanding of cardinality, subitizing, and problem solving among many other skills. Keeping in mind that everything is a learning process was important, I focused on the experiences and practice that the children would have. Having realistic expectations without underestimating children was key at the beginning. With continuous exposure and freedom to explore with their own methods of counting, children excelled at the tasks at hand. The representation of their collections was a challenge at times, as this required understanding of the quantity and fine motor skills. With practice and problem-solving skills, they became quite competent at the task. They soon found creative ways to organize collections into groups by sorting based on characteristics or small quantities. By focusing on the skills they do have, children feel successful and motivated to continue their learning. Having counting collections as a weekly activity never becomes a boring task. They are always eager and excited to count. They also transferred many skills into other activities throughout the day. They understand that everything has value including themselves. Breaking up into groups for specific activities becomes an easy task. Mathematical aspects become relatable to the children in their everyday life events. This is another way in which they now acquire understanding of the world. As a teacher, I have become more objective when observing and have found ways to guide my students.

—Natali Gaxiola, preschool teacher

At the preschool and kindergarten levels, supporting children's mathematical understanding involves building a foundation for the understanding and skills that will be developed later in their education. We want children to think that mathematics makes sense and that they can make sense of it, we want them to be able to use their knowledge to discover new ideas, and we want them to use their

growing knowledge to solve problems in ways that are consistent with their intuitive problem-solving strategies.

Learning from and with Children

Children come to school with mathematical experiences and knowledge. We have highlighted the details of children's thinking as a way of focusing on what children already know and are able to do. Teachers who have learned about children's thinking often find that their students know more than they have presumed. They recognize that part of focusing on what children know is learning to observe the details of children's strategies and learning to listen to how children describe what they are doing. Teachers also recognize that children participate in doing mathematics in varied ways. Part of understanding who children are and how they participate requires that we learn about and attempt to draw from the practices of their families and communities. A focus on children's thinking can help us to see not only what children know and are able to do mathematically, but also who they are as people.

Drawing on children's knowledge of counting enables students to leverage their informal knowledge in ways that help them develop their understanding of counting and problem solving and see themselves as capable mathematicians. Understanding counting supports children to operate on numbers, develop place value understandings, see and extend patterns, and so on. As children learn to count and extend those ideas to join, separate, compare, and group within their collections, they develop their ideas of what it means to add and subtract and even multiply and divide. They not only then make connections between these operations and counting collections, but they also connect their understandings of the operations to each other. They see how the same collection of 15 tops can be added to, taken away from, sorted, compared, and grouped.

Although we have focused our discussion on the development of foundational number concepts and operations, it is not our intention to suggest limiting the mathematical experiences of young children to only those elaborated upon in this book. We have considered in depth one strand of the mathematics to illustrate the importance of attending to the details of children's thinking.

Considerations for Your Teaching

Learning from and with children has implications for how you think about your teaching. Throughout this book, we have highlighted a set of principles that can guide your thinking about your practice.

- Look for what children know and focus on what they *can* do.
- Ask children about their thinking: how they figured it out, how they counted, how they solved that problem, and so on. There is no single right question to ask children to get at their thinking. Use your knowledge of children in general, the particular child, and their mathematical understandings to guide you.

- Ask children to share their thinking with each other. Support them to consider the ideas of their peers.
- Let children take the lead. Children need the opportunity to make sense of the mathematics in their own ways. They often do not think about the mathematics in the same ways adults do.
- Create space for children to get started. Let them struggle a bit; provide support, but try not to do all the mathematics for them. Recognize that not all children will count or solve problems in the same way at the same time.
- Change things up. Vary what children count, where they count, who they count with, and when they count. Try different kinds of story problems. Ask a range of different questions. This will support them to show you all that they know.
- Don't be afraid to try something new or something that you think might be more challenging for a child.

Teacher Reflection

My students share their thinking with each other in different ways—partners, small group, and whole class. Sharing gives kids opportunities to articulate their thinking, clarify ideas, ask questions, and explain/compare strategies used. Sharing thinking with each other helps kids see a problem from different perspectives and allows them to see a range of strategies that can be used to get to a solution. By seeing and listening to how others solve a problem, kids can start to reflect about their own thought process, revise their work, and/or adjust their strategies. They start to make connections and develop a deeper understanding of concepts.

—**Anne Tseng,** *kindergarten teacher*

Remember that we often underestimate what children can do. A focus on children's thinking supports us to continue to gain insight into the sophisticated mathematics that begins with our youngest learners.

Children's Thinking and Equity

A central goal of learning about children's thinking is for both teachers and students to see themselves as capable of making sense of and doing mathematics. Noticing and building from what children *can do* helps us to see the potential within children's incomplete or partial understandings. Viewing the world of mathematics from a child's perspective allows us to broaden ideas of what counts as mathematics, opening space for multiple ways of knowing and doing to emerge in classrooms.

Considering children's thinking in this way provides an entry point into striving for equity: seeing the varied knowledge and experiences children bring to school, drawing on those strengths and helping children to see themselves as capable, connecting their out-of-school experiences with their in-school experiences, and creating spaces for different ways of participating. Striving for equity also involves keeping in mind that the ways schools and society are structured will shape opportunities for children in classrooms. This includes how and what assessments are used, what resources are made available to schools and for which students, who goes to a school and what their histories and identities are, whose voices are heard and valued, and so on. So working toward equity requires attention to and pushback against the classroom practices that limit who participates and what is valued, as well as forces outside the classroom that create differential opportunities and limited views of whose ideas matter. It is our hope that beginning to see what children know and can do will enable each of us to challenge conceptions of who is seen as able to do mathematics in school. By striving for equity through the lens of children's thinking, we have the opportunity to redefine what it means to learn and succeed in school and to influence beyond the classroom walls the policies and practices that structure participation and opportunity for children.

APPENDIX: VIDEO FOCUS QUESTIONS

To access the online video clips:
You can scan the QR codes located throughout the book or go to www.heinemann.com and click the link in the upper right to **Log In**. (If you do not already have an account with Heinemann you will need to **Create an Account**.)

Register your product by entering the code: **YCMCGI**.

Once you have registered your product, it will appear in the list of **My Online Resources**. Click on the product to view the videos.

Video Name	Questions to Consider
2.1 Mohammad counts 8 bears	What do you notice about the order Mohammad follows as he counts the bears?
3.1 Miley's counting sequence	What happens after Miley is prompted to see if she can count past 11?
3.2 Miley counts pennies	How does Miley's number sequence while counting orally compare with the one she uses while counting the collection of pennies? What do you notice about her counting sequence when she gets to 20?
3.3 Logan counts pennies	What do you notice about Logan's counting sequence the two times he counts the collection?
3.4 James counts 8 bears	James counts his collection twice and gets different totals. What do you notice each time about his use of one-to-one correspondence?
3.5 Lily counts 15 bears, then 6	Lily counts her bears twice, and each time gets 14. Can you see what she does differently each time? What do you notice about her counting of 6 bears?
3.6 Milani counts 24 caps	What do you notice happens when Milani counts as she places the caps in a bag? How is this different from her previous counting?
3.7 Mia counts and recounts 15 bears	Mia counts her collection a second time and arrives at the correct number in her collection. What does she do differently the second time?

Video Name	Questions to Consider
3.8 Example of child who touches each object without saying number words **3.9 Example of child who counts some objects more than once**	See table (Figure 3.3) for details of each video segment.
3.10 Example of child who counts without touching objects **3.11 Example of child who skips an object** **3.12 Example of child with accurate one-to-one correspondence**	See table (Figure 3.3) for details of each video segment.
3.13 Fina counts 8 rocks	What do you notice about Fina's application of the cardinal principle? What do we learn from the follow-up question (asking her if she can give 5) about her understanding of cardinality?
3.14 Leonardo counts bears	What do you notice about Leonardo's application of the cardinal principle?
3.15 Example of child who does not count the entire collection	What might you ask to see if a child knew to count the entire collection?
3.16 Gracie counts 8 organized and then 8 unorganized bears	How does being required to organize the collection herself influence Gracie's counting?
3.17 Joshua counts and sorts 15 airplanes	How do the interviewer's questions support Joshua to organize and count his collection? How does counting the parts of the collection help him count the entire collection?

Video Name	Questions to Consider
3.18 Christian makes a set of 27 blocks	Christian counts and recounts because he is not sure he has the correct total. What do you notice about what supports him to get to 27?
3.19 Bryan counts 15 bears	What do you notice about how Bryan exhibits the different counting principles in this episode?
3.20 Sebastian counts out loud and then counts pennies	What do you notice about Sebastian's use of the counting principles as he counts pennies? How does his counting sequence differ from the oral count to the counting of the pennies?
3.21 Hazel counts 30 pennies	What do you notice about Hazel's use of the counting principles? What does her number sequence show she is beginning to understand about the structure of the number system?
3.22 Gracie counts 31 pennies	What do you notice about Gracie's use of the counting principles? What could you ask her next about the pennies that she has just counted?
4.1 Errington counts and separates airplanes	What do you notice about how Errington counts his collection? How does he figure out how many will be left if 6 fly away? Why do you think the interviewer asks him which ones flew away?
4.2 Sofia counts and separates bears	What do you notice about Sofia's counting of her collection? How does she figure out how to solve the problem?
4.3 Gracie counts, recounts, then separates bears	What do you notice about how Gracie counts her collection? How does she figure out how to solve the problem? What do you notice about the interviewer's questions?
4. 4 Christian counts and compares bears	How does Christian know that there are more green bears than red bears?
4.5 Aileen counts ears on bears	Aileen is able to solve what adults would consider a multiplication problem, even though she does not yet have a formal understanding of multiplication. How is she able to do this? What strategy does she use?
4.6 Hector shares crayons	Hector counted a collection of crayons that are in packages with 2 crayons each. How does he figure out how much each person will get if he shares them among 3 people? What do you notice about how he talks about the packages and the 3 piles?
4.7 Christian counts and joins bears	Christian had counted his collection of 15 bears. Where did Christian start counting to figure out how many bears he would have if we gave him 7 more bears? What strategy did he use?

Video Name	Questions to Consider
5.1 Birthday countdown	What other informal situations might present opportunities to mathematize young children's conversation?
5.2 Water table fill and spill	How does the teacher move in and out of play while supporting students' counting? What other questions might she have asked?
6.1 Daniel solves joining and separating problems	Can you identify the problems Daniel is asked to solve and the strategies he uses to solve them? What is the same about his strategies?
6.2 Mohammad solves a separating problem	What strategy does Mohammad use to solve his separating problem? What does he do with his fingers to support his solution?
6.3 Hazel solves a multiplication problem	How does the interviewer support Hazel to work on the problem without doing the math for her? How does Hazel solve the problem?
6.4 Mohammad solves a multiplication problem	How does Mohammad solve the multiplication problem? What do you notice about the yellow blocks in his stacks? How does he use what he knows about fives?
6.5 Math story time	See Questions for Further Reflection.
9.1 Christopher counts to 100	What do you notice about how Christopher figures out how to move through the decades? What does this suggest about his understanding of base ten?
9.2 Daniel counts pennies and makes tens	What do you notice about Daniel's counting? What does his counting reveal about his partial understandings?
9.3 Hector counts blocks and makes tens	A moment earlier Hector had counted the collection of blocks by ones. What do we learn about Hector's understanding that we would not have known if the interviewer had not asked him about numbers he likes to count by?

REFERENCES AND SUGGESTED READING

The ideas portrayed throughout *Young Children's Mathematics* are drawn from over thirty years of research and work with teachers. Cognitively Guided Instruction, which provides the basis for the ideas in this book and its companion, *Children's Mathematics*, draws on research-based knowledge of the development of students' mathematical thinking as a way to support teachers' classroom practice. CGI has been studied extensively. For the past eight years, we have been focusing more particularly on preschool and kindergarten teachers and students. Much of what we are finding in these studies parallels the work in early elementary school. Children at these ages know more than we often would expect. Teachers have shown how productively they can take up the details of children's mathematical thinking in both informal and formal spaces to support students' participation and learning. The list here is a sampling of the CGI-related research that supports the ideas in this book.

Carpenter, T. P. 1985. "Learning to Add and Subtract: An Exercise in Problem Solving." In *Teaching and Learning Mathematical Problem Solving: Multiple Research Perspectives*, edited by E. A. Silver, 17–40. Hillsdale, NJ: Erlbaum.

Carpenter, T. P., E. Ansell, M. L. Franke, E. Fennema, and L. Weisbeck. 1993. "Models of Problem Solving: A Study of Kindergarten Children's Problem-Solving Processes." *Journal for Research in Mathematics Education* 24 (5): 427–40.

Carpenter, T. P., E. Fennema, and M. L. Franke. 1996. "Cognitively Guided Instruction: A Knowledge Base for Reform in Primary Mathematics Instruction." *The Elementary School Journal* 97 (1): 3–20.

Carpenter, T. P., E. Fennema, M. L. Franke, S. B. Empson, and L. W. Levi. 2014. *Children's Mathematics: Cognitively Guided Instruction.* 2nd ed. Portsmouth, NH: Heinemann.

Carpenter, T. P., E. Fennema, P. L. Peterson, C. P. Chiang, and M. Loef. 1989. "Using Knowledge of Children's Mathematics Thinking in Classroom Teaching: An Experimental Study." *American Educational Research Journal* 26 (4): 499–531.

Carpenter, T. P., M. L. Franke, V. Jacobs, and E. Fennema. 1998. "A Longitudinal Study of Invention and Understanding in Children's Multidigit Addition and Subtraction." *Journal for Research in Mathematics Education* 29: 3–20.

Celedón-Pattichis, S., and E. Turner. 2012. "'Explícame qué tienes ahí': Supporting Mathematical Discourse in Emergent Bilingual Kindergarten Students." *Bilingual Research Journal* 35 (2): 197–216.

Fennema, E., T. P. Carpenter, M. L. Franke, L. Levi, V. Jacobs, and S. Empson. 1996. "Learning to Use Children's Thinking in Mathematics Instruction: A Longitudinal Study." *Journal for Research in Mathematics Education* 27 (4): 403–34.

Fennema, E., M. L. Franke, T. P. Carpenter, and D. A. Carey. 1993. "Using Children's Knowledge in Instruction." *American Educational Research Journal* 30 (3): 555–83.

Franke, M. L., T. P. Carpenter, L. Levi, and E. Fennema. 2001. "Capturing Teachers' Generative Growth: A Follow-up Study of Professional Development in Mathematics." *American Educational Research Journal* 38: 653–89.

Franke, M. L., A. C. Turrou, N. M. Webb, M. Ing, J. Wong, N. Shin, and C. Fernandez. 2015. "Student Engagement with Others' Mathematical Ideas: The Role of Teacher Invitation and Support Moves." *The Elementary School Journal* 116 (1): 126–48.

Jacobs, V. R., L. L. C. Lamb, and R. A. Philipp. 2010. "Professional Noticing of Children's Mathematical Thinking." *Journal for Research in Mathematics Education* 41 (2): 169–202.

Turner, E., and S. Celedon-Pattichis. 2011. "Problem Solving and Mathematical Discourse among Latino/a Kindergarten Students: An Analysis of Opportunities to Learn." *Journal of Latinos in Education* 10 (2): 146–68.

Wager, A. A. 2013. "Practices That Support Mathematics Learning in a Play-Based Classroom." In *Reconceptualizing Early Mathematics Learning*, edited by L. English and J. Mulligan, 163–81. Dordrecht, Netherlands: Springer.

Wager, A. A., and K. Delaney. 2014. "Exploring Young Children's Multiple Mathematical Resources Through Action Research." In *TODOS Research Monograph 3: Embracing Resources of Children, Families, Communities and Cultures in Mathematics Learning*, 25–59.

Wager, A. A., M. E. Graue, and K. Harrigan. 2015. "Swimming Upstream in a Torrent of Assessment." In *Mathematics and Transition to School: International Perspectives*, edited by R. Perry, A. Gervasoni, and A. MacDonald, 15–30. Dordrecht, Netherlands: Springer.

Wager, A. A., and A. N. Parks. 2015. "A Toolbox for Supporting Early Number Learning in Play: Moving Beyond 'How Many.'" In *Proceedings of the 37th Annual Meeting of the North American Chapter of the International Group for the Psychology of Mathematics Education*, edited by T. G. Bartell, K. N. Bieda, R. T. Putnam, K. Bradfield, and H. Dominguez, 828–35. East Lansing, MI: Michigan State University.

Wager, A. A., and K. Whyte. 2013. "Young Children's Mathematics: Whose Home Practices Are Privileged?" *Journal of Urban Mathematics Education* 6 (1): 81–95.

Be amazed by your students' mathematical thinking

Includes Extensive Online Video

Second Edition

Children's Mathematics

Cognitively Guided Instruction

Thomas P. Carpenter
Elizabeth Fennema
Megan Loef Franke
Linda Levi
Susan B. Empson

Heinemann
DEDICATED TO TEACHERS

Grades K–5 • 978-0-325-05287-8 • 2014

The second edition of *Children's Mathematics* is a landmark resource for knowing how your students think about math. Through decades of research and classroom experience, the authors have detailed Cognitively Guided Instruction: an instructional approach focused on students' mathematical thinking.

This bestselling book provides a comprehensive guide to posing problems that elicit student thinking, interpreting how students solve those problems, and coaching them to apply what they already know to new and more complex mathematical situations. Each chapter helps you anticipate student thinking, and a corresponding online library of more than 90 classroom videos lets you watch teachers interacting with students in various mathematical situations.

Includes access to more than 90 videos

"The more you listen to students' mathematical thinking, the more you will be amazed by what students can do."
—Thomas Carpenter, Elizabeth Fennema, Megan Franke, Linda Levi, and Susan Empson

Learn more at Heinemann.com/ChildrensMath

Heinemann
DEDICATED TO TEACHERS

 Houghton Mifflin Harcourt.

 @HeinemannPub